REFORMING THE NATIONAL SECURITY COUNCIL: EFFICIENCY AND ACCOUNTABILITY

HEARING

BEFORE THE

COMMITTEE ON FOREIGN AFFAIRS HOUSE OF REPRESENTATIVES

ONE HUNDRED FOURTEENTH CONGRESS

SECOND SESSION

SEPTEMBER 8, 2016

Serial No. 114–224

Printed for the use of the Committee on Foreign Affairs

Available via the World Wide Web: http://www.foreignaffairs.house.gov/ or http://www.gpo.gov/fdsys/

U.S. GOVERNMENT PUBLISHING OFFICE

21–460PDF   WASHINGTON : 2016

For sale by the Superintendent of Documents, U.S. Government Publishing Office
Internet: bookstore.gpo.gov   Phone: toll free (866) 512–1800; DC area (202) 512–1800
Fax: (202) 512–2104   Mail: Stop IDCC, Washington, DC 20402–0001

COMMITTEE ON FOREIGN AFFAIRS

EDWARD R. ROYCE, California, *Chairman*

CHRISTOPHER H. SMITH, New Jersey
ILEANA ROS-LEHTINEN, Florida
DANA ROHRABACHER, California
STEVE CHABOT, Ohio
JOE WILSON, South Carolina
MICHAEL T. McCAUL, Texas
TED POE, Texas
MATT SALMON, Arizona
DARRELL E. ISSA, California
TOM MARINO, Pennsylvania
JEFF DUNCAN, South Carolina
MO BROOKS, Alabama
PAUL COOK, California
RANDY K. WEBER SR., Texas
SCOTT PERRY, Pennsylvania
RON DeSANTIS, Florida
MARK MEADOWS, North Carolina
TED S. YOHO, Florida
CURT CLAWSON, Florida
SCOTT DesJARLAIS, Tennessee
REID J. RIBBLE, Wisconsin
DAVID A. TROTT, Michigan
LEE M. ZELDIN, New York
DANIEL DONOVAN, New York

ELIOT L. ENGEL, New York
BRAD SHERMAN, California
GREGORY W. MEEKS, New York
ALBIO SIRES, New Jersey
GERALD E. CONNOLLY, Virginia
THEODORE E. DEUTCH, Florida
BRIAN HIGGINS, New York
KAREN BASS, California
WILLIAM KEATING, Massachusetts
DAVID CICILLINE, Rhode Island
ALAN GRAYSON, Florida
AMI BERA, California
ALAN S. LOWENTHAL, California
GRACE MENG, New York
LOIS FRANKEL, Florida
TULSI GABBARD, Hawaii
JOAQUIN CASTRO, Texas
ROBIN L. KELLY, Illinois
BRENDAN F. BOYLE, Pennsylvania

AMY PORTER, *Chief of Staff*   THOMAS SHEEHY, *Staff Director*
JASON STEINBAUM, *Democratic Staff Director*

(II)

CONTENTS

REFORMING THE NATIONAL SECURITY COUNCIL: EFFICIENCY AND ACCOUNTABILITY

THURSDAY, SEPTEMBER 8, 2016

House of Representatives,
Committee on Foreign Affairs,
Washington, DC.

The committee met, pursuant to notice, at 10:00 a.m., in room 2172 Rayburn House Office Building, Hon. Edward Royce (chairman of the committee) presiding.

Chairman ROYCE. If we could ask all the members to take their seat and the audience as well, this hearing Reforming the National Security Council: Efficiency and Accountability, will come to order.

In recent years, there has been increasing bipartisan concern over the size and the role of the President's National Security Council. In too many cases, its traditional role of "honest broker" has evolved to a policy-making role. It has even undertaken secret diplomatic negotiations and that has been done outside of Congress' view.

Indeed, one observer recently wrote, "The national security advisor and his or her staff remain among the most influential entities in the Federal bureaucracy that are not subject to direct congressional oversight." This has proven to be a problem for this committee.

While concerns about the NSC aren't new, they have reached new heights, leading to current proposals before Congress to statutorily restrict the size of the NSC staff. This is a staff that has increased from 100 persons at the start of President George Bush's presidency to reportedly over 400 people today on the NSC staff. Such a large staff sends the message that the President intends to run foreign policy and military operations out of the White House to the exclusion of the cabinet.

It also makes for more meddlers. Indeed, former Defense Secretary Gates has complained that the "micromanagement" of the Obama White House "drove me crazy." A smaller staff would more likely empower cabinet secretaries to do what they have been selected and confirmed by the Senate to do and that is to run their departments.

More staff means more meetings and often paralysis. According to a report in the Washington Post last year, on some issues, NSC meetings of the cabinet deputies "grew so repetitive" that "deputies stopped coming, sending assistant secretaries and below in their stead." How many hearings has the committee held on Ukraine at which State Department officials have told us that the White House is still debating Kiev's request for heavy defensive weapons?

Also of concern, the profile of an NSC staffer has changed from a seasoned professional doing a stint at the White House as the capstone of their career, to that of junior professionals just off the campaign trail. As one interviewed for the Atlantic Council's Study we will hear about today said, "This is no place for on-the-job training of bright, young, but inexperienced people." Especially at the expense of the State Department.

Take the President's move to normalize relations with Cuba, secretly run out of the White House by two NSC staffers. Secretary of State Kerry was not informed of these negotiations until the discussions were well underway, and State Department officials in charge of the region found out only as the negotiations were all but done.

Why do we care? When the committee requested that these NSC staffers testify, we were told no and given a separation of powers excuse. But our role and the responsibility is to conduct oversight of U.S. relations with foreign nations. And if the committee can't hear directly from those most involved in these negotiations, our role and influence—and that of the American people we represent—is significantly minimalized.

This morning, we will hear from several witnesses who have direct experience with the growing size and role of the President's NSC. While today's focus is about process, process is important to good policy. And we hope that our discussion will lead to recommendations for the next administration to improve the efficiency of this important body.

And I now turn to the ranking member for any opening remarks from Mr. Eliot Engel of New York.

Mr. ENGEL. Thank you, Mr. Chairman. Thank you for calling this hearing. Ambassador Miller, Ambassador Bloomfield, Mr. Chollet, welcome to the Foreign Affairs Committee. We are grateful for your time and your expertise.

It has been nearly 70 years since the National Security Act created the National Security Council. Over that time, the council has proved to be a flexible and dynamic body. Every President has shaped the NSC staff in a way that has worked best for his purposes.

Congress intended for the NSC staff to serve as the President's advisory and interagency coordinated body. As the National Security Act put it, to "advise, coordinate, access and praise" policymakers relating to national security.

Obviously, over that time, national security politics and concerns has changed, as the world has changed and the NSC has had to keep pace. As we think about how the NSC might look under future administrations, we should keep in mind lessons learned in the NSC's first 70 years.

First, a selection of a National Security Advisor is one of the most critical appointments the President will make. This person sets the tone for the rest of the NSC and the National Security Agencies. The President should have full faith with the National Security Advisor as a trusted confident, a role that Congress has supported.

Secondly, the President's policy staff should be national security experts with experience managing interagency processes. Even though many of them are detailed from other parts of the government, their loyalty should be to our national security and not to any one agency or service.

And thirdly, while the NSC staff should certainly be in the business of advising the President on policy and ensuring the agencies are carrying out that policy, the NSC staff itself should not be carrying out the policy. That responsibility rests with the cabinet agencies with Congress' oversight.

It is essential to our discussion today how do we ensure that the execution of foreign policy stays where it belongs. One common explanation is that the NSC mission creep results from the NSC staff growing too large and the easy solution is to limit the size of the staff. I am sympathetic to that feeling because we don't want it to be too large and we don't want it to be usurping things that the State Department or the Agency should do. But it is not just that. That, in itself, in my opinion, is too simplistic. It fails to take into account why the staff is growing and ignores the bureaucratic demands placed in the NSC.

The real questions we should be asking are about the appropriate role of the NSC and how it is managed, issues that are important, regardless of the size of the staff. I do want to say that I am concerned about the size of the staff but I think these other things are at least equal of concern as well.

In a certain way, the NSC was set up as a clearing house. Seventy years ago, the cabinet agencies had relatively clear-cut missions with a minimal amount of overlap. When matters emerged that required cross-agency collaboration or tradeoffs, the question went up the food chain to the NSC and the NSC coordinated among agencies.

Today, we face so many more issues that are crosscutting and overlapping and they often involve a whole host of cabinet agencies. Just consider the Zika virus. State Department, HHS, and the Agriculture Department all have roles to play in addressing that problem but our civilian agencies are still essentially a stovepipe bureaucracy. So, when questions emerge about one of the many complex national security issues we face, those questions still get passed up to the NSC, often leaving policy-making decisions in the White House's hands. Over time, this pattern has forced the staff to grow as well. Past attempts to create so-called tsars to oversee overlapping issues have proved to be a Band-Aid at best, and at worst, totally ineffective. So, how do we empower our agencies to deal with a modern set of challenges without having their first phone call be to the White House? How do we modernize our agencies and, we think, decades-old bureaucratic structures ill-suited to the new challenges we face?

We know this sort of reform is possible. We saw it succeed decades ago when the Goldwater-Nichols Act forced our military services to work together in joint commands. That law promoted collaboration and a more unified approach to military concerns. Following the same approach, we need to make it easier for the talented men and women in our cabinet agencies to collaborate and arrive at policy consensus. That way, NSC staff could get back to their original mission, advising the President on policy, seeing that policy carried out, and facilitating coordination among agencies only in those instances when it is absolutely necessary.

Yet, we simply cannot expect our agencies to shake off decades-old procedures and habits if Congress isn't providing them with the tools and resources they need to become effective, modern organizations. It has been 15 years since Congress sent a State Department authorization to the President. I want to repeat that, 15 years since Congress sent a State Department authorization to the President. I don't think anyone on this committee, on both sides of the aisle, is happy about that. This committee recently marked up such legislation. It is sitting on the launch pad, waiting for House leadership to say go. I think the problem that we are discussing today is one more reason that the House needs to finish its work on the bill and I would encourage all the other National Security Committees to look at what needs to be done to bring their agencies into the 21st century.

To our witnesses: I am curious to hear your views on the structure of the NSC and how we can make our agencies more effective and collaborative when it comes to policymaking. Again, we are grateful for your time.

Thank you, Mr. Chairman. I yield back.

Chairman ROYCE. Thank you, Mr. Engel. So, this morning we are pleased to be joined by a distinguished panel. We have Ambassador David Miller. He is a Nonresident Senior Fellow at the Atlantic Council. Previously, Ambassador Miller served as the Special Assistant to the President for National Security Affairs at the National Security Council staff. Additionally, he served as the United States Ambassador to Zimbabwe and to Tanzania.

The Honorable Lincoln Bloomfield. Ambassador Bloomfield is chairman of the board of the Stimson Center and previously he held a series of positions in the Departments of State and Defense, including serving as the Assistant Secretary of State for Political Military Affairs.

And we have the Honorable Derek Chollet. He is Counselor and Senior Advisor for Security and Defense Policy at the German Marshall Fund of the United States and previously he served as the Assistant Secretary for International Security Affairs at the Department of Defense.

Without objection, the witnesses' full prepared statements will be made part of the record and members will have 5 calendar days to submit any statements or questions or any extraneous material for the record.

So, Ambassador Miller, if you could please summarize your remarks, we will begin with you.

STATEMENT OF THE HONORABLE DAVID C. MILLER, JR., NON-RESIDENT SENIOR FELLOW, THE ATLANTIC COUNCIL (FORMER SPECIAL ASSISTANT TO THE PRESIDENT, NATIONAL SECURITY COUNCIL)

Ambassador MILLER. Thank you, Mr. Chairman. It is nice to see you again.

Chairman ROYCE. Good to see you back.

Ambassador MILLER. We spent many interesting hearings on Africa, so it is great to be back.

Ranking Member Engel, thank you and all the members of the committee. I must say I am exceptionally pleased to see this many members of your body interested in the management of the NSC. It is an immensely serious topic. It doesn't get a lot of public discussion.

Chairman ROYCE. I am going to ask you, though, Ambassador, to move your microphone right there.

Ambassador MILLER. Does that work? Good. It is just a lack of practice. I will get it.

I am here today to present the Atlantic Council report, which I think you all have seen a copy of. It is named ''A Foundational Proposal for the Next Administration.'' It was drafted over a couple of years by Ambassadors Tom Pickering and Chet Crocker, myself, and Dan Levin. I suspect you know most of them and have talked with them before.

The report is meant to address two issues, that is, what did we learn over the 60 or some interviews we conducted over 2 years. The interviews were conducted by all of us in-person. We felt that the subjects that were being discussed were sensitive enough that when you interviewed former cabinet officers or national security advisors that those doing the interviewing had to have had similar jobs, sat in the same meetings, and been subject to the same pressures.

I must say that the opening comments were excellent and, in many ways, speak to our observations but let me offer a few comments on the spirit of our report.

We spent so much time on the NSC because if it doesn't work, it is like congestive heart failure. If the NSC is not working well, the entire executive branch foreign policy and military structure slows down and is not effectively used.

And there is another point that I would like to make at the outset and I hope will make throughout the presentation and that is, this is a non-partisan report. We looked at administrations going back for some period of time. General Scowcroft's thesis at West Point was on the Eisenhower NSC. So, we go back a good ways.

I am fond of describing the document as an owner's manual for the NSC. It tells you what has worked in the past, what has not worked, and it is policy neutral, if you will. It is meant to say if you want to run an NSC in a manner that has been effective in the past, take a look at this document. Learning how to run the NSC is something that we may have lost track of.

The recommendations are quite simple and they are coincident with what you two have mentioned in your opening comments. The NSC needs to get back to its original mission of coordinating policies for the President and then ensuring that those policies are faithfully executed. The role of the National Security Advisor is absolutely critical. It is clearly, I believe, the most important Presidential appointment not subject to Senate confirmation.

The size of the NSC staff has, as we have all observed, grown quite large. There are a variety of reasons for that but it is much larger than it has been historically.

The NSC has struggled, over time, with creating a strategic planning staff that has never worked too well and there are some issues about how to coordinate executive branch legal advice better.

In the few moments I have left, the chairman had a question about why this happened. I think to a certain degree, the most important factor is inertia. It has just grown. It has not been successfully checked by the Congress or by cabinet members or agency heads. There is another observation that the NSC has become in-box driven, that there are so many issues in the world that surely, the President must have a position on all of them. The 24-hour news cycle I think is another contributing factor. We have talked to senior NSC officials who said the ability to delegate key Presidential positions to departments and agencies to make public statements has not worked exceptionally well.

The State Department, where I enjoyed working and am proud to have worked with the foreign service, is still seen as being too slow, too bureaucratic and we all need to address that. The multi-disciplined threat that you have mentioned is another issue where the NSC has stepped in and added personnel to deal with that. And finally, there is an issue that I will touch on at the end and that is there seems to have developed a serious split in this town between politically loyal foreign policy professionals and professionals that work for the departments and agencies. I think we need to address that.

Finally, and I thought your comments about the lack of an authorization bill for the State Department were bang on. There is little reward in this town for building institutional capability in the executive branch. That is in some distinction from the private sector, where the building of institutional capability is seen as a key responsibility for a CEO.

I am over my time but I have one less thing I would like to say. I have been out of town for a little bit and when I came back and got involved in writing this, my friends said to me, David, you have been gone too long. I am in San Antonio. And the trust that was in this town when I was younger, which was some time ago, seems to have gone. And I hope this hearing is part of a step to begin to develop a more civil dialogue among those of us who may see issues differently but we all love the country.

That is it.

[The prepared statement of Ambassador Miller follows:]

Atlantic Council

BRENT SCOWCROFT CENTER
ON INTERNATIONAL SECURITY

LESSONS FOR THE NATIONAL SECURITY COUNCIL

The Hon. David C. Miller, Jr.
Nonresident Senior Fellow, Brent Scowcroft Center on International Security, Atlantic Council

House Committee on Foreign Affairs
Hearing: "Reforming the National Security Council: Efficiency and Accountability"
September 8, 2016

Introduction

Chairman Royce, Ranking Engel, and Members of the Committee:

I am very pleased to be here this morning, in particular to see Congressman Royce before whom I enjoyed testifying a few years ago on African issues. You are taking valuable time to discuss a very important issue: management of the National Security Council. While examining the management of the National Security Council (NSC) hardly grabs headlines, it is of great national importance.

I am here to present a report by the Atlantic Council's Brent Scowcroft Center on International Security. The report is entitled "A Foundational Proposal for the Next Administration" written by a core group composed of Ambassadors Tom Pickering and Chet Crocker, Dan Levin, a lawyer with extensive national security legal experience, and myself. The report is part of the Atlantic Council's National Security Council Reform Project. Copies of the report has been provided to your offices and I submit it for the record today. Rest assured that all of us involved with the report will be available to discuss with you and your staff members our observations for as long as you find it productive.

Our core group, with the help of many colleagues discussed, debated, interviewed, reflected, and wrote for almost two years. The Atlantic Council's Brent Scowcroft Center took our writing, added to it, improved it, and turned it into the report you have with you. In this process, we were superbly supported by the Council's Air Force Senior Fellow and special operations pilot, Colonel (select) Jason Kirby, who made a major contribution to the report you have received.

I expect that in the question period, you will want to concentrate on the recommendations of the report and our perceptions of why the National Security Council has seen its mission expand, and personnel grow, over the past few decades. So, let me take these few minutes at the outset to quickly review the procedure and intent of our writing.

The spirit of this report

First and foremost, let me emphasize at the outset that this is a nonpartisan report. It is not meant to be critical of any particular administration: neither the current one nor its predecessor, nor that administration's predecessor. Working at the NSC is tough, demanding, and frequently thankless. We mean this report to offer guidance going forward. It is not meant to criticize all who have worked hard in service of our country. To be specific, we have been in touch with the current leadership of the NSC who have offered helpful comments on our report and have taken some of our recommendations to heart.

Why did we spend so much time on the NSC?

If the NSC is not working well, it is like congestive heart failure. The Executive Branch's foreign policy, intelligence, and military structure suffers. To quote one of our most helpful, intelligent, and wise contributors: "Bad process beats good people nine times out of ten." Further, as General Scowcroft said in his foreword to the report: "Good structure does not guarantee success, but bad structure almost always overcomes good people and leads to poor results."

How would we describe this document?

I frequently describe this document as an "owner's manual" for the NSC. It describes in some detail the mission, procedures, practices, and staffing that has worked well for decades for many presidents faced with many crises. It also reviews shortcomings that have been widely observed in administrations when these accepted principles and practices have been ignored. The report is the distilled wisdom of many people who have served on the NSC going back to the Nixon Administration and Dr. Kissinger as the national security advisor.

How did we conduct the research?

Our core group—Tom, Chet, Dan, and I, supported by Colonel (select) Kirby—interviewed a very wide range of retired senior leaders: former national security advisors, military commanders, intelligence officials, as well as State Department and NSC officers. More than sixty are listed at the back of the report. I suspect that you know many of them well. The interviews were conducted by us in person as some of the discussions were sensitive and were best done among people who have shared the responsibilities and faced the issues discussed. It is important to remember that the recommendations you find in the report are not those of us in the core group, but the distillation of these interviews.

What was most striking about the results?

We were surprised—indeed, somewhat stunned—at the uniformity of views expressed by each of the "communities" that we interviewed. We interviewed political appointees from both parties and nonpartisan career officials. The uniformity of their observations and the vigor with which they were expressed were remarkable. If this had not been the case, had we simply found a random pattern of criticism, we would have stopped our work. It was the consensus of views that allowed us to make recommendations that we, and they, believe would improve the functioning of the NSC.

What are the recommendations?

Focus the National Security Council mission. The NSC should return to its original mission of managing the development of policy options for the president using the recommendations of the principals to optimize the use of diplomatic, economic, military, and intelligence resources. When policies are adopted, the NSC should coordinate implementation, provide support when necessary, and insure that the President's intent is being followed.

Define the national security advisor's role. The selection of the national security advisor is probably the most important appointment a president will make without the advice and consent of the Senate. The national security advisor must be compatible with the president and ideally should be a nationally recognized foreign policy and security leader with significant government management experience.

Reduce and restrict the size of the NSC staff. Limit the NSC staff to 100 to 150 professionals with the background and expertise necessary to execute their principal duties. Prior significant government and management experience should weigh heavily in the selection process. Multi-year service should be expected.

Designate a strategic planning staff. A key function of the NSC is the development of strategic plans for the president, monitoring their implementation, and giving the relevant department planning staffs representation on the NSC senior staff.

Use interagency teams and task forces. Recognizing new strategic threats and opportunities, the NSC should foster the creation of a limited number of interagency teams to deal with emerging multi-disciplinary strategic issues. These teams should be led by the appropriate Department or Agency that have the resources to execute the mission, and supported by NSC senior staff when required.

Coordinate legal advice. During times of crisis, there is significant pressure to receive legal advice supporting the president's policy in a timely manner, even if some relevant general counsel's offices are not included in the decision making process. The national security advisor should insure that the Office of Legal Counsel coordinates this effort. Speed can sometimes trump wisdom and legal precedent, leaving substantial legal confusion in the aftermath.

Prepare for a different transition. Preparations for the transition are underway. We would emphasize that, with the unusually "operational" nature of the current NSC, the records of operational accounts be shared with the incoming NSC team and personnel held over long enough to ensure continuity of key operational accounts.

Why has the NSC grown to its current size and mission?

1. Perhaps the most important factor is inertia. Beginning under President Clinton, the staff increased in size and scope of mission. This continued under President George W. Bush with the advent of 9/11 and its aftermath and has continued under President Obama. The "institutional inertia" has been unchecked by Congress or successfully resisted by relevant Cabinet Secretaries and Agency heads.

2. There is a general observation that the NSC has become "inbox driven." Increasingly, the president and NSC staff feel that the president should be "involved in" or "up to speed" and "have a position" on a very wide range of issues, many of which are seen as not being of strategic importance.

3. The 24-hour news cycle and social media environment has also led to a growth in the staff, as the White House believes that the challenge of agile and quick response to international news stories is required and attempts to delegate this function to Departments have been unsuccessful.

4. The State Department, accurately or not, is seen as being "too slow" or "too bureaucratic," which in turn leads to the NSC assuming more day-to-day management of important foreign policy issues. While there is considerable discussion of why this problem exists, it needs to be addressed.

5. The emergence of "multidiscipline" threats and opportunities require the creation of task forces comprised of multiple Department and Agency personnel. To date, there has been a tendency for these to be led by the NSC staff, rather than a lead Department, thus, once again, increasing the number of staff.

6. Although hard to quantify, the distrust between the "politically loyal" NSC staff and the professional officers in the Departments has led to the growth of the "loyal" NSC staff and sometimes a dysfunctional gap between Departments and NSC staff.

7. The lack of interest in, or reward for, building institutional capability in the Executive Branch also contributes to the growth of the NSC. The president can "get things done quickly" with the White House staff, which in turn leads to further Department deterioration.

How do you hope the report will be used?

We have written a good deal on each of the key recommendations. The document moves from General Scowcroft's introduction to the very succinct executive summary to much longer discussions of each key point. We have tried to capture the range of concerns and advice on each of the key recommendations in greater detail as we move through the document.

You will note that each recommendation is not something cast in stone. Presidents are elected to pursue their own policies and organize the White House in ways that work for him or her. Our recommendations are meant to offer guidelines based on decades of historical experience allowing an incoming administration to learn from the past as they consider the future.

What do you hope to accomplish?

There is a presidential transition coming up. Whoever wins, we hope he or she will pay careful attention to what we have gleaned from these interviews with so many who have led the country in these areas. You ignore history at your peril, and we have tried to capture many years of history in this report.

We also hope that this will help guide a Congressional discussion of relations between these two branches of government who share a responsibility for the management of our foreign and military policies.

If I may, a final observation. This body can lead an effort to restore trust among key players in the management of our foreign policy and military force projection. This intangible imperative is hard to describe. It cannot be legislated or created by organizational innovations. Trust comes from recognizing that all involved in this effort care deeply for their country.

Thank you, and I look forward to your questions.

Chairman ROYCE. Ambassador Miller, that is exactly the tone we want to set and we appreciate you being the lead witness here.

Ambassador Bloomfield.

STATEMENT OF THE HONORABLE LINCOLN P. BLOOMFIELD, JR., CHAIRMAN OF THE BOARD, THE STIMSON CENTER (FORMER ASSISTANT SECRETARY FOR POLITICAL MILITARY AFFAIRS, U.S. DEPARTMENT OF STATE)

Ambassador BLOOMFIELD. Thank you, Chairman Royce, Ranking Member Engel. Thank you, members of the committee, for the honor of testifying before you today. I would like to second the remarks that both of you made. And it is clear that the issues that are covered in my prepared testimony are the same ones that you have already articulated.

I really want to make four brief points from the standpoint of someone who does not have the most recent experience and has not served on the NSC but, in the last 35 years, I have been in the interagency in five different administrations. So, I am going to take a broader view.

I will play the resident optimist. I think everyone who is here in this room today is here because they believe that it can be fixed and so do I.

The first point starts with the legal mandate for the NSC and the privileges that the NSC enjoys. So long as the NSC staff and the national security advisor are coordinating the work of the other national security agencies of government and following the legal mandate to make the tools of government more integrated and more effective, military and non-military, then they should continue to enjoy the prerogative of being the President's staff and, therefore, not being Senate-confirmed, not being subject to testimony, not having their paperwork subject to the same oversight and public oversight that the line agencies of government have.

That said, there are lines that they can cross, and have in the past, where these privileges come into question. One of the two sources that I consulted, and I applaud the effort of the Atlantic Council and its co-chairs, both of whom I greatly respect, but I have in my hand the so-called Tower Commission Report. And people of a certain age will remember this big blue book that I am holding. This was one of the eight investigations on the Iran-Contra Affair. This was done by three very respected statesmen, Senator John Tower, Senator Edmund Muskie, and Lieutenant General Brent Scowcroft, who had previously served as President Ford's National Security Advisor. They found that the NSC Advisor and staff had conducted a covert operation in transferring funds to the Nicaraguan contras. And without re-litigating the merits of the case, they issued a warning to future Presidents, which I will read to you. They are warned, and members of the National Security Council and National Security Advisors, "of the potential pitfalls they face, even when they are operating with what they consider the best of motives."

So, I think that there is a cautionary note. There may be issues where the NSC is becoming operational and setting policy, rather than coordinating it. And that is, historically speaking, a problem.

The second source and the third point I want to make has to do with the evolution of the NSC and, with the privilege of the committee, I would like to hold up a book by my late father, MIT Professor of Political Science Lincoln Bloomfield, who served on the NSC under his colleague, Zbigniew Brezezinski, for 1 year under the Carter administration and wrote in 1982 ''The Foreign Policy Process: A Modern Primer,'' in which he reviewed 40 years of National Security Councils.

Among the insights gained here were that technology moves only in one direction. Under the Kennedy administration, the White House Communications Agency installed equipment so that the White House could see the same diplomatic dispatches, the same military dispatches, the same intelligence reports as the other agencies, which made them more powerful and brought them into the conversation.

Under the Nixon administration, they had secure facsimiles. So, now, the White House could send agendas and papers for discussion in the situation room. And Dr. Kissinger famously used this to great effect, and was actually dual-hatted as Secretary of State and NSC Advisor for 2 years.

And so, in some ways, you can't turn the clock back to the 1970s or '80s, or the 1950s, and we have to recognize this.

But before we conclude, and this is my final point, that the NSC needs to be—that there is a right size for the NSC and that the President's prerogative should be, in some way, changed or interfered with by the Congress. I think it is really important to recognize that the NSC is trying to chase a bureaucracy in Washington that is much bigger than it was 20 or 30 years ago. There are so many more undersecretaries and assistant secretaries and issue-specific offices that they are asked to coordinate that you could understand why the size has gotten larger. And I think this leads to, perhaps, a broader conversation on how to right-size the entire national security process.

I published last Friday, in Foreign Policy, an article that takes a slightly larger view of the national security management challenge and I commend it to the members, I think copies have been made available, and with the chairman's permission and the ranking member, I would hope perhaps it could be brought into the official record or the hearing.

Chairman ROYCE. Without objection.

Ambassador BLOOMFIELD. Thank you, sir.

[The prepared statement of Ambassador Bloomfield follows:]

Ambassador Lincoln P. Bloomfield, Jr.
Chairman, Stimson Center

September 8, 2016 hearing on "Reforming the National Security Council:
Efficiency and Accountability"
U.S. House of Representatives Committee on Foreign Affairs

Chairman Royce, Ranking Member Engel, Members of the Committee, thank you for the honor of appearing before you this morning. I have served as a foreign policy official in five previous administrations, including various positions with the State Department, the Defense Department and the Office of the Vice President. Although I have not worked on the NSC Staff, hopefully my experience over the past 35 years will assist the Committee's deliberations.

The advice I offer today may be summarized as follows:

1. There is no correct size and structure of the NSC Staff, and its measure of effectiveness is how well that entity suits the President's deliberative style and needs. The NSC Staff is the President's personal staff, and in theory at least, it is for the President alone to determine if the NSC staff is right-sized and functioning well.

2. That said, it is fair for others to judge how effectively the NSC, and the NSC Staff, are coordinating the policies and programs of all Departments and agencies involved in national security. The National Security Act of 1947 is clear that the formal body designated as the National Security Council – meaning the President, Vice President, and Secretaries of State, Defense and Energy, joined at NSC meetings by statutory advisors and non-statutory invited principals – is advisory in nature. Its function is to integrate policies affecting national security for the purpose of achieving effective coordination. If problems are arising with interagency coordination, that is a legitimate oversight matter for Congress.

3. Because it is the President's staff and is not subject to the congressional accountability and public records access that apply to legally authorized agencies of government, there is a "red line" the NSC Staff should not cross, namely conducting operations and implementation of Executive branch policies.

These latter two points – that the NSC, and NSC Staff, exist to improve the coordination and effectiveness of national security policy, and that they must avoid stepping into operational and implementation roles – are areas where problems can and do arise.

In addition to my own experience in government, I have found two sources of information on this subject very instructive. First is the Report of the President's Special Review Board, the so-called Tower Commission report, co-authored by Senators John Tower and Edmund Muskie and Brent Scowcroft in the wake of the mid-1980s Iran-Contra scandal, where proceeds from covert US arms sales via Israel to Iran were "diverted" to fund the Nicaraguan contra rebels. While the Tower Commission report of February 26, 1987 is of course dated, its conclusions on the appropriate role of the NSC and NSC Staff are sensible and illuminating, as I will explain.

The second source, if the Committee will permit me this privilege, is one of the fourteen books authored by my late father, MIT Professor of Political Science Lincoln P. Bloomfield, who served for one year as Director of Global Issues working on President Carter's NSC Staff under his longtime academic colleague Zbigniew Brzezinski. Prof. Bloomfield's 1982 book The Foreign Policy Process – A Modern Primer chronicles the evolution over time of the role and functions of the National Security Advisor and NSC Staff.

The November 1986 revelation that President Reagan may have authorized weapons transfers to Iran as a *quid pro quo* for releasing Americans taken hostage in Lebanon became a wider scandal when the Attorney General announced that funds from the arms sales may have been diverted to the Nicaraguan Contras. As the Tower Commission report details, the National Security Advisor and members of the NSC staff had taken "direct operational control" (IV-1) over covert action activities including funding for the Contra rebels that Congress had prohibited DoD, CIA and any other agency or entity "involved in intelligence activities" from doing under the second so-called Boland Amendment of October 3, 1984.

As the report concluded (IV-3):

"Even if it could be argued that these restrictions did not technically apply to the NSC staff, these activities presented great political risk to the President. The appearance of the President's personal staff doing what Congress had forbade other agencies to do could, once disclosed, only touch off a firestorm in the Congress and threaten the Administration's whole policy on the Contras."

I cite this not to revisit past controversies but to highlight the "pitfalls" about which the Tower Commission endeavored to "warn future Presidents, members of the National Security Council, and National Security Advisors...even when they are operating with what they consider the best of motives." (I-2) I would expect anyone who lived through the Iran-Contra affair in detail, as I did, to endorse the view that policy advisors serving as the President's personal staff and operating under the privileges and protections accorded out of respect for the President's zone of internal deliberation, should stick to advising the President and coordinating interagency policy development. They cannot cross the line into the arena of official actions and operations, which are the responsibility of agencies fully empowered and answerable to the Congress and the public, and expect to retain their immunity from external accountability.

There are issues today where the White House should keep this admonition in mind. The Administration's recent release of a previously classified 2013 Presidential Policy Guidance document setting out the process for determining who will be targeted by lethal UAV (or 'drone') strikes and for authorizing such "targeted killings," as these have come to be termed, was in response to widespread concern at home and abroad. As the April 2015 updated report of the Stimson Task Force on US Drone Policy had concluded, any use of lethal force, in order to meet the test of democratic legitimacy, must satisfy standards of oversight, accountability and transparency. As expedient as it may seem to have the NSC staff formulate detailed security options for the President and manage their execution, the President's interests will be better served by keeping the NSC staff strictly in an advisory and coordinating role.

This will not be easy in 2016. While there are enduring lessons from the past, today's NSC operates in an environment much different from the days when President Kennedy relied on 10-15 NSC staff advisors, or even when President Carter had an NSC staff of 35. As Prof. Bloomfield noted in his Primer, President Eisenhower used the NSC to run a highly structured interagency coordinating process so that the President would have visibility over the policies and operations of the State Department, Pentagon and CIA. During the Kennedy Administration, after the White House Communications Agency established an independent capability to receive the same military, intelligence and diplomatic information as other agencies, the NSC staff was better able to generate its own policy advice for the President, and has done so ever since.

Once secure facsimile communications links were established during the Nixon Administration between the White House and other departments and agencies, the NSC was further empowered to set the agendas and dictate the policy review and development process for the relevant Departments and agencies. Dr. Henry Kissinger used this capability extensively, achieving such dominance over foreign and security policy that President Nixon made him Secretary of State, and Kissinger held both positions concurrently for more than two years. By contrast, LtGen. Brent Scowcroft kept a low profile with a small but elite staff, and is widely admired for the way he facilitated very effective government-wide policy coordination under both Presidents Gerald Ford and George H.W. Bush.

Over time, whatever advantages the State Department once had over the White House in maintaining a superior grasp of foreign policy events has eroded. Foreign officials and Ambassadors stay in close contact with the NSC Staff, and its members attend international events of importance along with State Department officials. Both have access to the same intelligence and cables from Embassies and military commands. With the growth in the size of the NSC Staff, the question to explore is whether its function is evolving from a policy coordinating role to a more specialized policymaking role, preempting the traditional functions of the State Department and the Office of the Secretary of Defense.

Is there a new reason for concern, or are changes in the NSC function simply a reflection of leadership style? Presidents have differed widely in their operating styles, and National Security Advisors have differed widely in their level of visibility and in the competitive or collaborative nature of their relationships with the Secretaries of State and Defense. The size of the NSC staff has also varied considerably; and yet, because it is far larger today than perhaps at any time since 1947, the potential disadvantages make this fact a legitimate focus of congressional scrutiny.

I conclude with two thoughts:

1. First, the NSC Staff and National Security Advisor, no less than the formal cabinet-level National Security Council itself, must never lose sight of its mandate under the 1947 law, which says (of the NSC): *"The function of the Council shall be to advise the President with respect to the integration of domestic, foreign, and military policies relating to the national security so as to enable the military services and the other departments and agencies of the Government to cooperate more effectively in matters involving the national security."* That is the NSC's *raison d'etre*: to help integrate the policies of all agencies, and to enable the military and others to cooperate more effectively – to be, as many have termed it, "an honest broker" among the national security players in the government. Can several hundred people serve effectively as an "honest broker"?

2. Before concluding that today's NSC is operating in a manner inconsistent with its legal mandate, I would raise the possibility that problems of effective policy coordination extend well beyond the NSC. It is true that former Cabinet members and other veteran policymakers of this Administration have complained of NSC staff micro-management. However, in looking to "right-size" the NSC Staff in its coordination role, Congress should not overlook the impact of so many new Under Secretary and Assistant Secretary positions added within the Departments of State and Defense in recent years, not to mention single-purpose envoys and issue coordinators. Homeland Security is a major new player in the national security community, as is the Directorate of National Intelligence. As I wrote in Foreign Policy on September 2, a serious management problem exists across the interagency space, with a splintering of issue portfolios along with uncontrolled inflation of subcabinet positions. A well-considered consolidation and streamlining effort with the full participation of Congressional oversight committees would bring many benefits. Surely one would be to make it easier for a future President to restore the NSC function to a form more closely resembling the lean operations run by Brent Scowcroft, Colin Powell and other well-regarded National Security Advisors.

I thank the Committee for this opportunity to offer perspectives on the NSC role and size, and would be pleased to respond to any questions.

Chairman ROYCE. Mr. Chollet.

**STATEMENT OF THE HONORABLE DEREK CHOLLET, COUN-
SELOR AND SENIOR ADVISOR FOR SECURITY AND DEFENSE
POLICY, THE GERMAN MARSHALL FUND OF THE UNITED
STATES (FORMER ASSISTANT SECRETARY FOR INTER-
NATIONAL SECURITY AFFAIRS, U.S. DEPARTMENT OF DE-
FENSE)**

Mr. CHOLLET. Mr. Chairman, Ranking Member Engel, members
of the committee, it is an honor to appear before you again and I
will briefly summarize my longer statement for the record.

I approach this important topic from a unique perspective. I
served on President-elect Obama's NSC Transition Team 8 years
ago and then I went on to serve for 6 years in the Obama administration at the State Department, at the Pentagon, and at the National Security Council staff at the White House. So, therefore, I
follow the assessment of this administration's NSC system with
great interest, since I both experienced and am partly responsible
for many of the concerns that have been raised.

Consider the three most common concerns expressed about the
current NSC. First, that it is too big; second, that it is too operational; and third, that it has a proclivity for too much micromanagement and too little strategic thinking. And let me take each
in turn.

First, most experts and former officials believe that the NSC is
too big. We certainly thought so during the 2008 transition from
President Bush to President Obama, as does the current NSC leadership today. And yet the trend, I think, is headed in the right direction. Today's NSC policy and leadership staff consists of fewer
than 200 people. And my understanding is that with the current
downsizing underway, and there has been about a 15-percent cut
in NSC staff since January 2015, the NSC staff size that Obama
will leave next year will be roughly the same as what he inherited
from President Bush in 2009.

And it is important to consider these numbers in context. Some
of the widely cited higher numbers of the Obama NSC staff size reflect the back office functions like those staffing the White House
situation room, the records management personnel, as well as the
integration of the Homeland Security Council in 2009. And moreover, even despite its growth, the current NSC remains comparatively small. The Joint Chiefs of Staff is over seven times larger.
The State Department's Office of the Secretary is nearly twice the
size of the NSC staff, as is the staff of the Congressional Research
Service. So in many ways, the NSC's evolution reflects global complexity and how much the world and our Government has changed.

For example, the traditional regional policy offices, Latin America, Asia, Europe, et cetera, have looked similar in both size and
function during the past several decades, yet there are now new
policy dimensions the NSC must cover such as cybersecurity, climate change, WMD proliferation, biosecurity and global health,
global economics, counterterrorism. Few of these issues were
prominent a quarter century ago and none of them reside in a single agency, which is why close coordination is so important.

Because of this complexity and the importance for the President to maintain flexibility in how she or he can respond to events, I believe it is a mistake to impose arbitrary caps on the NSC staff size, nor do I believe it wise to make the position of National Security Advisor require Senate confirmation. And here, I can do no better than echo the 1987 Tower Commission Report, which studied this issue carefully and in its warning that doing so, making the NSC Advisor Senate-confirmed would undermine the Presidential advisory role the National Security Advisor must play and only create more bureaucratic confusion and tension than it would resolve.

Now, concerns about the NSC size relate directly to a second enduring critique that the NSC is too operational. Now, agencies must be given the responsibility and be held accountable for doing their jobs. And in my experience, that is what Presidents and members of the NSC staff wanted. But at the same time, agencies must operate within the policy parameters set by the President. Now, sometimes, when the White House tried to enforce regular order and place the agencies in charge of a policy, then it was accused of taking its eye off the ball. And where you stand often depends on whether you agree with the policy direction. For example, Obama's NSC has held tight control over U.S. troop levels in Iraq and Afghanistan but it is important to remember that the Bush White House conducted the same intense oversight when managing the surge in Iraq from the West Wing in 2007 and 2008. Moreover, some policy issues lend themselves to a strong White House lead and many of those delicate tasks require such agility that they are best managed from a tight circle within the White House.

Yet, these must be the exception, rather than the rule, which brings us to the third common critique, that by micromanaging, the NSC is not doing enough strategy.

I used to run the strategy office at the NSC. So, I can fully appreciate how difficult this task can be. And in today's tumultuous policy environment where our President is expected to respond to almost everything instantly, it is very difficult to keep the urgent from overwhelming the important. Crisis management tends to dominate the NSC's operations. And although during my time and since, the NSC staff worked very hard to allow senior officials the opportunity to think about long-term strategy and examine cross-cutting issues, it has not nearly been enough.

Mr. Chairman, Ranking Member Engel, members of this committee, the recent focus on the NSC's design and operation has generated an important debate. I welcome congressional attention to this issue. My hope is that by opening up this conversation, we can make some necessary changes, empower agencies to do their jobs, while ensuring that the President gets the advice and support she or he requires to conduct a strong, coordinated, and strategic national security policy that serves the interest of the American people.

Thank you very much and I look forward to your questions.

[The prepared statement of Mr. Chollet follows:]

Prepared Statement for the Record

"Reforming the National Security Council: Efficiency and Accountability"

Derek Chollet

**Counselor and Senior Advisor for Security and Defense Policy,
The German Marshall Fund of the United States**

**Committee on Foreign Affairs
U.S. House of Representatives
September 8, 2016**

Mr. Chairman, Ranking Member Engel, members of the Committee, it is an honor to have this opportunity to appear before you again. As we approach this November's election and prepare for a new Administration taking office next year, it is a good time to assess our government's national security decision-making process – what works, what needs improvement, and what innovations may be required.

I approach this topic with the perspective of participating in the recent national security decision-making process from all sides – having served on President-elect Obama's NSC transition team eight years ago, then for six years in the Obama Administration at the State Department, Defense Department, and on the National Security Council Staff at the White House. Therefore, I've followed the assessment of this Administration's NSC system with great interest, since I both experienced and am partly responsible for many of the critiques one hears.

The NSC is the engine room of U.S. national security and foreign policy. As the president's closest national security staff, it leads and coordinates the interagency process. It integrates policy across agencies to ensure coherence. And it is the key mechanism to implementing the President's priorities across the government. To perform such essential roles, the NSC must be strong, effective, tightly-focused, and well-managed. This is a tough task, and no Administration's process has ever worked as well as the experts – and many officials – believe it should.[1]

Consider the three most common complaints one hears about the current NSC: first, that it is too big; second, that it is too operational and does the work Agencies should do; and third, that it has a proclivity for too much micro-management and too little strategic thinking.

---

[1] This statement draws on Derek Chollet, "What's Wrong With Obama's National Security Council?" *Defense One*, April 26, 2016; and Derek Chollet, *The Long Game: How Obama Defied Washington and Redefined America's Role in the World* (PublicAffairs, 2016).

The NSC staff has become larger – it has nearly doubled since 1992, and this trend has been steady under presidents of both parties.[2] Most experts and former officials believe that the NSC is too big. We certainly thought so during the transition in 2008 – and the current NSC leadership believes so today. Yet as of now the trend is headed in the right direction: today's NSC policy and leadership staff consists of fewer than 200 people, of which almost 90% are civil servant detailees. And my understanding is that with current downsizing underway (there has been a 13% staff reduction since January 2015), the NSC staff size Obama leaves next year will be roughly the same as what he inherited from President Bush in 2009.

It is crucial to consider these numbers in context. Some of the widely cited higher numbers of the Obama NSC staff size reflect the "back office" functions like those staffing the White House Situation Room, as well as the integration of the Homeland Security Council in 2009. Moreover, even despite its growth, the current NSC remains comparatively small – the Joint Chiefs of Staff is over seven times larger, the State Department's Office of the Secretary is nearly twice the NSC's size, as is the staff of the Congressional Research Service.

It is also important to understand what's behind this growth over the past few decades. It is not just bureaucratic ballooning or a turf-grab. In many ways the NSC's evolution reflects global complexity, and how much the world – and our government -- has changed. During the George W. Bush years, when the U.S. government underwent structural innovations in an attempt to address new threats (such as the Director of National Intelligence or the Department of Homeland Security), the NSC changed as well, a trend that has continued under Obama.

For example, the "traditional" regional policy offices – Europe, Asia, Latin America, etc. – have looked similar in both size and function during the past several decades (there are some exceptions, especially concerning the Middle East and South Asia). Yet there are now new policy dimensions the NSC must cover, such as cybersecurity, climate change, WMD proliferation, biosecurity and global health, homeland security, global economics, and counter-terrorism. None of these issues reside in a single Agency, which is why close coordination across the government is so important.

Because of this complexity – and the importance for the President to maintain flexibility in how she or he can respond to events – I believe it is a mistake to impose arbitrary caps on the NSC's staff size. Nor do I believe it wise to make the position of National Security Advisor require Senate confirmation. Here I can do no better than echo the 1987 Tower Commission in its warning that doing so would undermine the presidential advisory role the National Security Advisor must play, and only create more bureaucratic confusion and tension than it would resolve.[3]

---

[2] Specifically, the NSC staff grew 28% under President Clinton, 38% under President George W. Bush, and thus far 16% under President Obama.

[3] As the Tower Commission concluded, "confirmation would tend to institutionalize the natural tension that exists between the Secretary of State and the National Security Advisor. Questions would increasingly

Concerns about the NSC's size relates directly to a second common critique: that the NSC is too operational, getting into the business of other government agencies, stifling the process with too many taskings and meetings and, at times, inappropriately assuming the lead.

Agencies must be given the responsibility for doing their job – and in my experience, that is what Presidents and those on his NSC staff wanted (which is why it is so frustrating when many key Agency officials get held up in the confirmation process). But at the same time, Agencies must operate within the policy parameters set by the President. So in many ways, such frustrations are inherent, as every White House struggles with managing the rest of the government. In my experience and close observation of Administrations of both parties, I've found that White House officials (whether civil servants or political appointees) tend to approach the bureaucracy in one of two ways: believing it is doing too much and going beyond what the president has decided, or that it is doing too little and not fulfilling what the president wants done.

The answer to both is more oversight – whether by meetings, taskings, and questions -- which can sometimes evolve into bureaucratic overreach. Even when a White House tries to focus more on the strategic issues and leave tactical implementation to the Pentagon or State Department, the process seems to gravitate back to the Situation Room. Given that the President will be the one held accountable by the public, press, the Congress, and the American people, the incentives usually are for the White House to take more control, not less.

Sometimes, when the White House tries to enforce "regular order" and place the agencies in charge of a policy, then it is accused of taking its eye off the ball and abdicating leadership (one hears this in many of the complaints about the Obama Administration's handling of postwar Libya in 2011). And of course, where you stand often depends on whether you agree with the policy direction. Take, for example, the use of the military. Yes, on behalf of the President, the Obama NSC has held tight control over U.S. troop levels in Iraq and Afghanistan. But it is important to remember that the Bush White House conducted the same intense oversight when managing the surge in Iraq from the West Wing in 2007-08.

Moreover, some policy issues lend themselves to a strong White House lead. For example, the White House has dominated U.S. policy toward China since the days of Kissinger. As George W. Bush's National Security Advisor, Stephen Hadley, recently put it, "the China account is so important that it requires a whole-of-government approach, which can only be coordinated by the White House."[4] And many of the most

---

arise about who really speaks for the President in national security matters. Foreign governments could be confused or would be encouraged to engage in 'forum shopping'…if the National Security Advisor were to become a position subject to confirmation, it could induce the President to turn to other internal staff or to people outside the government to play that role."

[4] See David Ignatius, "In Kissinger's footsteps, Susan Rice steers smooth U.S.-China relations," *Washington Post*, September 1, 2016.

delicate tasks require such secrecy and agility that can only be managed by a tight circle at the White House (the planning for the Bin Laden raid or the diplomatic opening to Cuba in 2014 are prime examples). Yet these must be the exceptions rather than the rule.

Which brings us to the third critique: that by micro-managing, the NSC is not doing enough strategy.

As someone who ran the NSC's strategic planning directorate during 2011-12, I can attest to the difficulty of keeping one's eyes on the horizon while there is such turmoil right in front of you. Especially in today's tumultuous policy environment, where a President is expected to respond to almost everything instantly, it is very difficult to keep the urgent from overwhelming the important. Crisis management tends to dominate the NSC's operations, particularly in recent years. Although during my time (and since), the NSC staff has worked to allow senior officials the opportunity to think about long-term strategy or examine cross-cutting issues, it has not been nearly enough.

But there is another element of the NSC's role in the design and coordination of national security strategy, which relates back to the question of oversight. There is a structural imperative for the White House to assert itself, especially when the President is trying to execute a strategic move. A firm hand on the tiller is required to implement a policy that is sustainable and precise, and often that can only come from the White House. To be clear, that does not mean that the NSC should be the lead in implementing the strategy. But on behalf of the President, I believe it is an essential part of the NSC's role to hold Agencies accountable for progress and to help ensure that decisions do not throw the policy off-course.

Mr. Chairman, Ranking Member Engel, members of this Committee, the recent focus on the NSC's design and operation has generated an important debate about the making of America's national security policy and the proper role of the NSC in that process. I welcome Congressional attention to this issue. My hope is that by opening up this conversation we can make some necessary changes, empower Agencies to do their jobs, while ensuring that the President gets the advice and support he requires to conduct a strong, coordinated and strategic national security policy that serves the interest of the American people. Thank you, and I look forward to your questions.

###

Chairman ROYCE. Thank you, Mr. Chollet. I think the difficulty here, if we look at the drift, is if we look Ambassador Miller's report, the report that we are discussing, in that report there is a story of a four-star general receiving a phone call with orders from a low-level NSC staffer. So, the directive did not originate from the President. It didn't originate from the Secretary of Defense. It didn't originate from the chairman of the Joint Chiefs. It originates from a rather low-level staffer.

Clearly, the goal here is to get back to a system on foreign policy that works when different agencies and branches play their proper role. What we have to figure out here is how to get a situation where diplomats do the negotiating, where commanders call in the air strikes, where Congress conducts oversight and that is not happening under the current and past. The way in which this has morphed over the years has led to these problems that we are talking about today.

And so, I would just ask this question to the panel: What State Department reforms are most necessary to facilitate the evolution of power from the NSC back to the Department where the expertise lies and where you don't end up with low-level staff members making these kind of calls to four-star generals? How do we get back to the system the way is intended to work and in which it will function most effectively?

And Ambassador Bloomfield, maybe you will add to that because you make the point that this has become a problem not just at the NSC but also it is something that affects us, Congress, and the administration. We have a situation where our instinct is to appoint a special position on everything and so you have all of the special envoys and all of the coordinators adding to the complexity of a situation where the agency that is supposed to be in charge of making the decision isn't doing its role.

So, I will open that question to the panel.

Ambassador BLOOMFIELD. If I may, Chairman Royce, I don't believe that the people who strategized American policy during the height of the Cold War, when we were 25 minutes from extinction from Soviet nuclear weapons, were any less intelligent than the people that we have in senior positions today. In fact, I would argue that we have too many very talented people trying to chase authority, funding, control over policy, authorship of policy. And I have many friends on the inside who have great difficulty getting a well-considered, innovative idea all the way out of the building in the State Department.

And so I think that consolidating offices, and this is under both administrations, Republican and Democrat. I have spent half my career outside the government. When I had been appointed to come in, I asked the question how much sense does this activity make? Is this something that we need to be doing, that my people should be spending time on, or are we just playing ping pong inside the bureaucracy and sending papers back and forth?

So, I think there is a great deal of process that can be consolidated. And what happens when you try to show how important an issue is by putting a special office in charge is that everything else becomes diluted. You dilute the currency of high-ranking people so that, in the Congress, you have 40 plus assistant secretaries. I was very honored to be an Assistant Secretary of State. If I were Secretary of State today, I don't think I could name them all or recognize their faces. These are Senate-confirmed——

Chairman ROYCE. Right. Well, there is another element of this. And that is part of this goes to the experience or the expertise of the staff. One of the questions in this study, the explanation from another lower level staff member is you have a hard time running the interagency process if you have never held a senior position in one of the agencies. So, this is another aspect of the problem, in terms of the expertise and not consolidating this decisionmaking where it belongs.

Ambassador BLOOMFIELD. If I may, at the high levels, the under secretary level. There was one Under Secretary of State under President Kennedy, that was the second-ranking person in the department. The President would call the Under Secretary on the telephone. There are six or seven today. The same in the Pentagon in the Office of the Secretary of Defense. And I think, by the way, the Office of the Joint Chiefs, the Combatant Command Staffs, I was there when they started to put joint JIACs together and was part of the approval process. They are thick with all sorts of flavors of experts on their own staffs. I think we need to downsize. And what happens is, you have high officials who only have one-seventh of the picture. How strategic of a view will an administration have if everyone has just a sliver or a soda straw view of policy that they care about? We need to start elevating people and giving them a broad swath of policy authority so that they can think very strategically and when the Zika virus becomes a problem, we can put a task force together and have it expire once the problem is under control.

Chairman ROYCE. Well, my time has expired, so I will go to Mr. Engel. But it seems to me the NSC should return to its original mission of managing the development of policy options for the President of the United States. If that can be the end game here, I think we can get back to its original function and an effective function. Mr. Engel.

Mr. ENGEL. Thank you, Mr. Chairman. I want to echo my concern along with you, the two questions you asked about the role of Congress. We are very anxious. Many of us feel that more and more things are slipping away from what Congress is supposed to do and we don't like it and don't think it is good for the country. So, I am very concerned about it.

I believe the chairman also spoke about tsars. And I wanted any of you who care to say what observation would any of you make about the usefulness of these tsars, the proliferation of special coordinators and special representatives that the State Department, these were created to shepherd initiatives into provide help with the coordination. And sometimes it has actually been an impediment to coordination. So, from the perspective of the NSC, do these types of structures help or inhibit effective interagency coordination? Anyone who cares to answer that?

And let me say, before you do, I want to thank all three of you for excellent testimony. And Dr. Miller, I am glad that you couldn't have put it better when you said that there is difference of opinion way all over the country and I think that is important.

The chairman and I have tried to conduct this committee as the most bipartisan committee in the Congress because we believe that foreign policy is bipartisan and differences need to stop at the water's edge.

So, I just want to let you know that in the 4 years we have been doing this, we have tried very hard. It doesn't mean we agree all the time, but we have tried very hard to work together. And my commendation to members, my colleagues on both side of the aisle, who have worked very hard, even when we have a disagreement, we have a good discourse and we try to find common ground.

So, if anybody wants to answer that tsars question, I would appreciate it. Ambassador Miller.

Ambassador MILLER. I ended up——

Mr. ENGEL. If you could, pull the microphone toward you.

Ambassador MILLER. I will get this. I ended up supporting one of our first tsars, when Bill Bennett was given the drug war. And so I have spent a good deal of time figuring out what support from the White House is appropriate and where it is damaging.

We, I think, have gotten to rely too much on Band-Aids and we appoint tsars, or special envoys, or administrators, when they are duplicative of functions that already exist but don't seem to be moving as fast as the White House would like or performing exactly what the White House wants.

So, my sense is that you need task forces. You need special envoys on occasion but your first examination ought to be is there an assistant secretary that already has this responsibility? Is there a competent Ambassador on-site? Because when you appoint a person with duplicative authority, it can really set things back. It is just confusing.

That said, there is going to be a need for these, as we go forward, but they ought to be led by the departments and agencies that have the lead stake in the issue and supported by the NSC.

Mr. ENGEL. Thank you. Mr. Chollet, you had your hand up. I don't know——

Mr. CHOLLET. Yes, well I very much want to echo what the Ambassador has said. Tsars have been, in the past, a good thing but there is also too much of a good thing. And the tsars that I, both at the State Department or at the White House that I worked closely with during my time in government, whether going back to the Clinton administration, the tsar on the Balkans, or during the Obama administration the SRAP structure on Afghanistan and Pakistan at the State Department, were successful, had some challenges, but were successful in trying to bring about greater coordination both within the Department. It is also within the broader interagency. But clearly, every administration, I think, in the modern era has seen a proliferation of these tsars. And when a new team comes in—we certainly did this in 2008, I expect the next transition team will do the same—is take a close look at these various idiosyncratic bureaucratic structures that administrations create, sometimes for personnel reasons, sometimes because an issue becomes so important that they don't want it to overwhelm the other senior officials who have the whole world to worry about. But I think we have to be very mindful moving forward that there can be too many of these and this will just create Band-Aids that don't actually get at the core coordination strategic problem that we are all interested in trying to solve.

Mr. ENGEL. Ambassador Bloomfield.

Ambassador BLOOMFIELD. Yes, if I may. My last position in government was as a special envoy in 2008. I came back part-time on an issue that the chairman knows about. I was to try to travel the world and quietly remove shoulder-fired missiles from circulation. And you had to be able to speak to heads of government, chiefs of defense, because no second in a ranking would ever give up a weapon, you have to go to the top. And so I took my orders directly from Steve Hadley and Condoleezza Rice and had very strong support from the NSC Counterterrorism Team. My observation, though, and this is a little bit of dirty laundry, is that there are lots of senior people walking the halls of the State Department looking for a job that is at their rank and that this is a way. They want these positions. It is not clear to me they are all necessary.

What I would do, and this is probably a little bit out of the ordinary but I have seen it in the past, is to identify prominent Americans in the private sector and in Congress who could be a well-received envoy to deliver a message to a head of state, somebody of prominence. And I include members of the House and Senate in that list on both sides of the aisle, which would add credibility to the President or the Secretary of State's message.

So, I hope we think about that and move in that direction.

Mr. ENGEL. Thank you. If the chairman will indulge me, I have a quick question that I would like to ask you, all of you.

The current House language in the fiscal year 2017 NDAA calls for Senate confirmation of a National Security Advisor if the NSC staff exceeds 100 employees, including detailees. I want to quote Stephen Hadley, who is former NSA to President George W. Bush. He said, and I quote him, "If a President thought that what he or she shared with the National Security Advisor could be compelled in public testimony, the President would look elsewhere for a national security and foreign policy confidant." That is a quote.

So, do you think that Senate confirmation, any of you, of the National Security Advisor would inhibit this person from serving the President and does it also raise questions about the constitutional separation of powers?

Anyone care to try it?

Ambassador MILLER. I suspect I speak for all of us but I will start off. And that is I don't think advice and consent for the President's personal staff makes sense.

That said, we are in a situation where the Congress needs to play a larger role and have a larger discussion with the President about how the NSC works and who is selected. Now, that doesn't mean a vote but I surely wish that you all and the Executive Office of the President have a more candid or active discussion about who is there and who is serving.

Mr. ENGEL. Thank you.

Chairman ROYCE. If the gentleman would yield.

Mr. ENGEL. Yes, certainly.

Chairman ROYCE. From my standpoint, if you look carefully at the language, the intent there seems to me, and it is not our language, it is from the Armed Services Committee, but the intent seems to be to control the size of the staffing and get it back to the original numbers because confirmation isn't required, as long as the executive branch concurs with evolving back to the original size of the indices NSC staff.

So, I don't think the intent is to drive confirmation. I think the intent is to try to exercise some kind of congressional oversight or control over what has actually happened in the agency. So, I would just throw that in for the mix. I don't know how else to do that but this hearing is an attempt.

Ambassador Miller?

Ambassador MILLER. I think if you look at what we have written, indeed, there is very strong support for limiting the headcount at the NSC, as it is seen as the root cause of a number of subsets of problems. But there is equally strong opposition to the advice and consent. So, I think your observation is right on.

Chairman ROYCE. Yes, I think it is a clumsy attempt to get at your objective. So, our hope is to reach a bipartisan consensus of a more effective way to get to that objective.

We go now to Ileana Ros-Lehtinen of Florida.

Ms. ROS-LEHTINEN. Thank you so much, Mr. Chairman. Thank you for this hearing. From the ransom payments in Iran, to the alleged secret Iran deals, and humanitarian catastrophe that is unfolding every day in Syria, the manipulations of intelligence on ISIS, there are too many examples of how the White House has manipulated information while keeping the Congress and, most importantly, the American people in the dark.

And Mr. Chairman, thank you so much for bringing up Cuba in your opening statement because that is a good example of what was happening with the secretive nature. The White House decided to keep not only Congress in the dark but also cut out the State Department and others, even though the White House was negotiating with the Cuban regime for more than a year. Then Assistant Secretary Jacobson testified before our committee in February 2015 that she found out about the negotiations just weeks before the announcement. And when former Deputy National Security Advisor and now Deputy Secretary of State Tony Blinken testified at his confirmation hearing in November 2014, he assured the Senate Foreign Relations Committee that any change in U.S. policy toward Cuba would be done in full consultation with Congress. Well, that turned out to be an utter falsehood, as less than a month later with zero consultation with the Congress, the administration announced what has proven to be a complete failure of a deal with the Castro regime. And as we heard from Ambassador Bloomfield, NSC staffers shouldn't conduct official actions, which are supposed to be the responsibility of agencies that are answerable to Congress, and then expect to be immune from accountability.

So, Mr. Chollet, I have a series of questions. We won't have time to answer them but maybe we can have a discussion afterward.

Is it worrisome that NSC is not accountable to Congress or that when Congress attempts to exercise our oversight authority in the foreign policy realm, it cannot perform that function because NSC officials do not testify before Congress? Also, what steps can Congress make in order to make the NSC more transparent?

There was a time when NSC staffers were trained on the proper rules to delineate between the duties and roles of the NSC and the duties and roles of the State Department or Defense Department, making sure that they didn't overlap and, instead, stayed focused on their responsibility in those lanes and left the policymaking to the proper person. And I was wondering if you received that kind of training when you were at the NSC and do you have any idea if training programs of this type still exist.

Also, in November of last year, when I traveled to Afghanistan and our generals on the ground indicated that their hands were tied when it came to operations, no doubt it was because, I believe, NSC was overriding our leaders on the field, and former Defense Secretaries Gates and Panetta both have complained about NSC staff imposing themselves on their jurisdiction. Based on your experience in both the NSC and various government agencies, maybe you can help shed some light on that.

Thank you, sir.

Mr. CHOLLET. Thank you very much and I would be happy to follow up with you as well, if I don't get fully to answer your good questions. First, I will take it in reverse order.

On the tension between White House oversight, political oversight, and what is going on in military operations, I experienced that on both sides of the ball, right, at the NSC staff but then also when I served at the Pentagon as an Assistant Secretary.

And whereas there are examples, and I don't know exactly when the example that the Ambassador's report cited about when a junior staffer apparently called the Pentagon to ask for something that was completely out of order, that is not the regular order. That doesn't happen that often, at least in my experience. And when it does happen, it should be stopped, absolutely. The National Security Advisors I have worked for, the Secretary of Defenses I have worked for would not tolerate that.

That said, there is such a thing as Presidential control over the use of military force. So, if the NSC staff, on behalf of the President, is essentially ensuring that the agencies follow the President's prerogative on how that force should be used, what kind of targets we hit, what sort of operations we conduct, it seems to me that that is something we would want.

I was struck in 2008 coming into the Obama administration how intensively the Bush White House and the Iraq/Afghanistan tsar and the directorate that was created to run the surge in Iraq, in particular, how deeply involved in military operational issues that that team was, much to the distress of uniformed military and the Secretary of Defense at the time to have a sitting three-star general working in the basement of the West Wing, essentially running the surge in Iraq.

So, I think that should be the exception. It should not be the rule, which then gets back to the opening question, which was NSC staff, senior NSC officials engaging in direct foreign engagements. I think there should be as little of that as possible.

Throughout our history, we have seen National Security Advisors take on important missions on behalf of the President that are extremely sensitive and secretive. Henry Kissinger's opening to China——

Ms. ROS-LEHTINEN. Thank you. That is right.

Mr. CHOLLET [continuing]. Brzezinski's normalization of China several years later. But then we have also as the Tower Commission pointed out, very negative examples of that.

Ms. ROS-LEHTINEN. Well, thank you.

Mr. CHOLLET. So, it should be the exception, not the rule.

Ms. ROS-LEHTINEN. Thank you very much. Thank you, Mr. Chairman. I know I am out of time but thank you for this hearing. Thank you, gentlemen.

Chairman ROYCE. Thank you. We will go to Mr. Brad Sherman of California.

Mr. SHERMAN. Last century the high-water mark for the NSC was Kissinger. Everything we complain about now was probably more true then, in terms of the NSC.

As to this century, I have seen this committee and the House of Representatives in general go from foreign policy makers to foreign policy kibitzers that are at least allowed to provide some oversight and some input to really an irrelevancy because the most important people making and carrying out foreign policy don't even come here and pretend to listen to us.

Mr. Chairman, the Armed Services Committee passes an authorization bill every year and nothing illustrates the importance of that more than that the provision to limit the size of the National Security Council is in their bill and will be considered in their bill, whereas our bill for 15 years is an exercise in—well, often isn't even written. It usually isn't even considered by the House and hasn't reached the President's desk in 15 years.

So, what we need to do is say not how can we possibly get the most important Presidential advisor on foreign policy to come into this room but how can we write an authorizing bill in this room that becomes law? And I would like to see us demand that we don't appropriate money for foreign policy that isn't authorized. And we could do that by insisting that the authorizing bill that we pass be joined to the appropriations bill and that neither the Senate nor the President should be able to get the money without dealing with the authorizing provisions. And if we, as a committee, would demand that the rule for considering the foreign operations appropriations bill include both the authorizing and the appropriation. And I would like them to be separate bills but separate bills where one of them is thrown away, that is not the best approach. So, if they were married, then, when they go over to the Senate, we make it plain—you have to have an authorizing and an appropriations bill. You go to the President and you say you want the money, you have to look at the appropriations; you have to look at the authorizations as well.

Mr. Chollet, I am going to go into a much less significant point. You compared the NSC staff to CRS. Is that just the CRS foreign policy national security folks? That is not their folks on medicine or transportation or whatever.

Mr. CHOLLET. Fair enough. I used the most expansive numbers both for the NSC staff——

Mr. SHERMAN. Right.

Mr. CHOLLET. So, I took the most number of them as well as CRS to try to make an apples to apples——

Mr. SHERMAN. But you looked only at what portions of CRS?

Mr. CHOLLET. No, no, no, no. This was the entire thing.

Mr. SHERMAN. Okay, so you are saying that——

Mr. CHOLLET. So, this is——

Mr. SHERMAN. But I mean it is like you are comparing apples with a fruit plate.

Mr. CHOLLET. So, I included in the NSC staff the back office people.

Mr. SHERMAN. Yes, but everyone at the NSC staff deals with national security. There are people over at CRS who are dealing with health policy. So, the fairer comparison would be the entire White House and the old Executive Office Building, and all the offices of the President, and all the tsars. Because otherwise, you are comparing a department at CRS that deals with health policy and you don't have anybody at—I hope you don't have anybody at the NSC who is focusing on a cure for cancer or——

Mr. CHOLLET. But there are people on health policy.

Mr. SHERMAN. On health?

Mr. CHOLLET. I mean not domestic health policy but global health is a huge issue.

Mr. SHERMAN. Right, global, yes. Okay.

Ambassador Miller, were you indicating a desire to say something?

Ambassador MILLER. My hope is that you all can take a very serious look at improving the performance of the State Department. I spent most of my life investing capital and looking at the performance of companies. Sometimes they are good, sometimes they aren't. But whatever, you can learn a lot.

State needs to step back. You need to help them step back and say what do we need to do to make the department work. The Foreign Service is a fine, fine institution. I was immensely well-served as a political appointee in two Embassies, very well served at the NSC. There is more human capability at State going to waste than in almost any institution I have ever seen.

Somehow or other, we need to put our minds together to say how can we fix this because——

Mr. SHERMAN. So you think maybe Congress should oversee the State Department, write an authorization bill, pass it into law, and have an agency of the Federal Government act according to congressional authorization. That is a brilliant and innovative idea, one that we ought to apply to the State Department.

And I yield back.

Ambassador MILLER. I have waited all these years for that opportunity. Thank you.

Mr. SHERMAN. I yield back.

Mr. ROHRABACHER [presiding]. Well, here we are and it is in my hands. There you go. Be afraid. Be very afraid.

All right, let me just note that I had the privilege of serving in the White House for 7 years and I had a lot of experience with the NSC and a lot of experience since then and during that time, with the other agencies of government. So, I have more than just having been here on this side of the questioning.

Let me suggest this. I think that our Government isn't working as effectively as it could and should. I think that targeting the NSC is the wrong target. Having, as I say, experience with all of these players, it is not the NSC that is the problem. The problem is we have a bloated State Department and a bloated intelligence community. I mean after 9/11, what did we do? We made the intelligence community even more complicated, put even another layer of bureaucracy between the President and his intelligence sources. That is what we did in Congress.

Now, the fact is the National Security Council was established so that the President of the United States would have people on his staff who could keep up on the issues of the day. And now there is a debate whether or not the NSC is overstepping its bounds when the President actually engages in foreign policy activities that I guess the Congress or other people or the State Department feels they should be conducting. Let us note that Kissinger made a dramatic difference in the history of this country when, at the height of the Cold War, when it was going against us, it looked like the United States was going down, that he changed the whole dynamics by reaching out to China. That happened secretly. I believe if they tried to do it through the State Department, that initiative never would have succeeded. That would have been undercut and every step of the way, not to mention what would happen if the CIA and everybody else was involved in it.

Let me note also that the bad use of the NSC, what Ambassador Bloomfield mentioned was the Iran-Contra Affair. We had given the contras $100 million the year before to the CIA and then all of a sudden we are going to cut them off. There is a lot of politics being played on that that culminated, instead of letting those guys go, Ollie North took it upon himself to make sure they got money for ammunition, et cetera. So, I don't think that is an example of how things go haywire.

And thinking back, the Iran-Contra Affair demonstrated that the President of the United States has to be a player in these things and has to have a staff that is able to be a player.

Ollie North, also, I might add, when he was there, took it upon himself to reposition a carrier battle group so that when the Achille Lauro was taken over that we would have airplanes that could actually intercept the terrorists when they were captured, if you remember that.

Now, I don't know if we would have gone through the normal channels whether that carrier battleship would force but they at least paid attention when Ollie North called up the admiral and said, that would be a good place to have put them there in case of emergency.

One personal example I remember and I have been deeply involved in the Afghan thing since I was a speechwriter. What is a speechwriter doing being involved in helping the Mujahideen in Afghanistan? But that is the way it was and there was a situation where a general called me and said look, we have to take off within a matter of days or there is a field hospital that will not go to the Mujahideen on the border of Pakistan and Afghanistan.

And these are men who put their lives on the line for us and the Pakistanis are demanding money for our planes to land and our planes aren't going to land. And thus, hundreds of Mujahideen are going to die because we don't have this field hospital that is in the back of the C-130 waiting to go there. Can you do something?

Now, at that time, I am a member of the President's staff. I am a Special Assistant to the President of the United States. Well, if I had to go call up somebody over at the State Department, the CIA, or the Defense Department, it would not have gotten done. I know that. Hundreds of people fighting for us against the Soviet army would have been dead. And I called up a guy at NSC and he said well, we can't do this on our own; I can't do this. And I said look, all I want you to do is take a call, give a call to our Embassy in Pakistan, and they will then tell the Pakistani Government that the White House has called and the job will get done. Oh, I can't do that on my own. You know what? He called back and he said okay, I will do it. Because I told him, I said okay, hundreds of people will die who are our best allies in the fight against the Soviet Union and they will die because you are not willing to make one call.

He calls back and says okay, I will do it. And do you know what? One call and that hospital equipment got there and hundreds of lives were saved. We need to have a National Security Council that can function, that can do that, that can save the lives of those of hundreds of thousands Mujahideen fighters or whoever it is that is in jeopardy around the world.

And isn't NSC involved in crisis management? Okay, the President needs a staff to be there during a crisis. Does the President need someone for policy analysis so that he is not getting hundreds of reports from different points of view? Let somebody be there who can digest it over a matter of days, rather than an hour when the President has to make a decision. No, we need that.

And I think that the NSC should not be decreased and, instead we should try to make the rest of the government more efficient and that is where things are breaking down.

Please feel free to comment on anything I just said right down the line, Ambassador Miller.

Ambassador MILLER. On the intel situation, I could not agree more. For my 2 years at the White House, I ran the Counter Terrorism Coordination weekly meeting, the CSG, Lincoln and I got to meet each other then.

Counter terrorism requires a very tight turning radius and that means speed of movement and trust of communicators. You can't do that among large bureaucratic structures I don't think. Eventually, it gets down to does the J3 trust you? Does the head of counter terrorism at the CIA trust you? Do your principals trust you as the first line actors? And if they don't, you can lose that advantage of information which may be stale in 2 or 3 days and you have to move.

On your ability to call, let us suppose you need to call the J3. The problem with a very, very large White House staff is that senior officers at the Pentagon don't get to know the White House staff and they don't really know who is phoning. And you get more stories about the White House called—456-1414 is not a self-dialing machine. You know——

Mr. ROHRABACHER. Ollie did make telephone calls.

Ambassador MILLER. Listen, I followed Ollie on and Ollie and I traded notes on a lot of stuff. I got to know the J3 well enough, General Scowcroft and Secretary Gates way back then. We all trusted each other. And you could pick up the phone and you could call then Admiral Owens, who was Secretary Gates' military aid, and say Bill, we have a problem and we have to do something in a hurry. Now, Bill knew who I was.

If you don't have that trust, things don't work right and that is one of the problems with having a larger staff. If the larger staff stays inside and does analytic work, that is fine. But if you are a special assistant, somebody at the Pentagon better know who you are when you pick up the phone and say let us move a carrier task group. That is a serious decision.

Mr. ROHRABACHER. All right, thank you. And real quickly, I am sorry I blabbed on with too much time here, but very quickly, if you have some disagreement, please feel free.

Ambassador BLOOMFIELD. Congressman Rohrabacher, I just want to reiterate the importance of the structure of government that has worked so well. The NSC staff should be up to the President. The President should have whatever staff the President is comfortable with, he or she, so long as the staff does not do things which would more properly be under the purview of both the American people's right to have oversight and the Congressional oversight and the authorized activities. As long as they are coordinating and operating under the 1947 mandate, they can have as many people as they want—whatever makes the President comfortable—but that line should not be crossed.

The second thing I need to say—Derek has been an Assistant Secretary of Defense, and I was in ISA for 8 years at the Pentagon—the National Command Authority is sacrosanct. There is a famous story in the Nixon administration when Dr. Kissinger called Secretary of Defense Laird and said the President wants such and such to be done. And he said well, let the President call— click. And that is the National Command Authority.

If there are lives on the line and exigencies, if you haven't predelegated the authority to the people who are capable of doing the right thing, whether it is the State Department in a Benghazi situation or the Pentagon in a military situation in the field, then that is a failure of policy, but it is fixable. We just simply need to recognize these are the things that have made America work so well in the past. We just simply need to recognize the lines and execute properly.

Mr. ROHRABACHER. Mr. Chollet.

Mr. CHOLLET. I know you are out of time, so I will be very brief. I fully agree with what both of my colleagues here have said.

I just want to echo, sir, your point, which is mainly the growth of the NSC does reflect the growing complexity and size of our national security apparatus and that there are entire dimensions of policy that didn't exist 25 years ago that now the President needs to fully understand. He needs to have folks around him who fully understand. So, that explains a lot of the growth.

I think the NSC is too big. I think it can be smaller and I think the trend, as I said, is headed in the right direction but I don't think we should have an arbitrary cap on it.

Mr. ROHRABACHER. Yes, I don't ever remember getting a briefing on the threat of cyber-attack back during the Reagan years.

Mr. Sires, you are now recognized.

Mr. SIRES. Thank you, Mr. Chairman. It is all right that you went over a little bit.

First of all, this is a very informative hearing. I want to thank you for being here. On one side we have experience, on one side we have youth that has worked, and Ambassador Bloomfield, you are in the middle somewhere, as far as—but it has been informative.

And from what I gathered, I would tend to think that the NSC is just too large. I have problems thinking that a staffer can call a four-star general and say, "Do this." To me, that is—I guess I have been involved in politics a long time and it is not your enemies that get you in trouble but your friends or people that work for you. And I think that that is a very possible scenario and it has happened. But as it gets larger, I think it is even more something that can happen and I have a problem with that.

I have a problem with the NSC negotiating. They negotiated secretly. We had here people from the State Department and we asked them about certain negotiations, especially with Cuba. And I don't know if they wanted to lie or not but we were told that they weren't negotiating when, in reality, there was negotiations going on. And I would think that if they are negotiating secretly and you have a State Department person come before this committee and you ask them the question, and she will say no, they weren't, I would take it at her word that she didn't know that secretly somebody was negotiating. And to me, that is a problem.

We are a State Department. We are very careful with people who are capable of doing the kind of work that some people at the NSC is doing. I also think that sometimes this committee, the NSC, is used as a buffer. This is to keep people away from reaching maybe the presidency or the President using the committee to keep other people away. There has got to be somebody in-between to absolve any responsibility.

So, I really don't think that keep growing this committee is going to be helpful to this country or is going to be helpful to the President. I think, as Ambassador Miller expressed, there are many capable people working in different places in the State Department where they are tripping over each other to do something. And they could do some of the work, instead of growing this committee.

And can you just tell me what you think it started to go wrong with this committee, this NSC committee? Where did you see that it started going wrong, with your experience? When did it take the wrong direction? Let me put it this way.

Ambassador MILLER. A very inelegant answer is that apparently over time, within the 18 acres at the White House, a sense that speed of movement was critical. And that goes way back, if you look at the graphs here, it goes way back to the Clinton administration, which we saw our first very big spike in NSC staff.

The illusion from my standpoint is that speed of movement is more important than wise decisionmaking. Wise decisionmaking is frequently slow and difficult and there are many times in which speed of movement is the most important issue that you are looking at. But it has become an excuse, I think, for not involving institutions that seem to move too slowly, that have a lot of wisdom and experience. This study began more than 2 years ago when I called some of my agency friends who had been involved in the Afghan situation and I said, really, nobody talked to you about what we were doing in the Middle East. And the answer was no, nobody talked to us. And I said you have got to be kidding me.

So, I don't have an elegant answer to that but I think one thing is that the White House has pushed on an open door. The Congress has allowed this to occur and it is not healthy for the Congress and it is not healthy for the White House either.

Ambassador BLOOMFIELD. Congressman, could I just say that I think this suggests a larger solution? I know people have specific complaints about the NSC staff, probably in both administrations, Republican and Democratic. Part of it is not their fault because with the tools and information they have, with the real-time media contacts, with Ambassadors coming and calling at the White House as well as the State Department and possibly visiting military dignitaries, the question arises of what can the State Department do that the NSC staff can't do. There is a little bit of ''we can do it all here.'' And part of it is because of technology and just the press of business.

So, I think without blaming people, we can look at that and say what can we do. Because if it goes much further, it does cross the line where there is no oversight and Congress can't call them before—they can't confirm the appointees. And the President should not want that to happen.

So, there needs to be a conversation. I, personally, think that Congress has immense power over the next President that could be a subject of discussion during the transition, and before knowing the result of the election, that has to do partly in the Senate with the confirmation process and partly with the amount of hearings and questions for the record. These are things which are enormous burdens on an incoming administration. If their appointees are going to be slow to be confirmed, if they are going to get thousands of questions that the bureaucracy will be tied up answering, you have something to bargain with. And this might be, Congressman Engel had brought up the question of, an authorization bill. I would like to see a grand bargain, where there are fewer high officials in the Executive Branch and frankly, maybe a few fewer gavels in the Congress so that we can get back to a leaner, high-level, principal-to-principal process.

My congressman is yelling at me. I will stop.

Mr. SIRES. Thank you very much.

Mr. CONNOLLY. Would my friend just yield for one quick observation?

Mr. SIRES. Sure.

Mr. CONNOLLY. Because I want to return to this when it is my turn. Ambassador Bloomfield, excellent point but I want to make one point. The change up here with respect to the NSC came out of the military, not the State Department. And that causes me grave concern about the dismissal of Young Turks calling a four-star and daring to ask or tell something. That is not a good enough reason to revamp the entire national security apparatus of the

President of the United States, which I think my friend, Mr. Rohrabacher, was making as well.

So, I want to engage in that when it is my turn but I think it is important to remember the genesis of the proposed change in the legislation. It didn't come out of the Foreign Policy Committee on the Hill. It came out of the Armed Services Committee.

And I yield back.

Ambassador BLOOMFIELD. Well, if I may, Congressman Connolly, I never thought of myself as an old codger but I know a lot of four-stars, retired and some active duty, and it has been my privilege to know them. And I have seen them during situations where they may even not take guidance from the Secretary of Defense on certain things, like ROE in a situation where they need to keep the peace the first day of an intervention. I know these folks and I have been there. Derek will have his own experience.

It is unfathomable to me that a four-star commander in the field would take guidance from a staffer in the bureaucracy. It is unfathomable to me. I don't understand it.

Mr. ROHRABACHER. Mr. Chollet.

Mr. CHOLLET. Just very briefly, I agree with that. And again, my experience is that that is a rare occurrence, where there is a junior staff who tries to call a four-star or a lieutenant colonel working in the NSC who calls an admiral to move a carrier battle group. It is an exception and not the rule.

Just one very quick observation on this question of oversight. When I served at the White House, I always found myself toggling back and forth between two perspectives. One is, why aren't the agencies doing what the President has decided? So, he decided to do something. Why isn't this happening or why is it happening too slowly? Or it is, what are they doing? The President hasn't decided yet. They are creating facts on the ground before the President has been able to actually make a decision on what he wants to do.

And I never found a way out of that dilemma, personally. And so I do think that there is a sort of secular trend toward greater oversight because, of course, that is the common answer for both. You hold more meetings. You do more taskings. You try to hold agencies accountable. And I think in some ways it goes back to this issue of we ultimately do hold the President accountable. When things go wrong, the President is blamed. When things go right, the President gets credit. And so the NSC staff as an extension of the President tends to be more involved in the policies and tasks.

Mr. ROHRABACHER. Well thank you very much. And that means that the President has to be accountable for what his appointees do or her. There you go.

Mr. Perry.

Mr. PERRY. Thanks, gentlemen. Thanks for all of you for being here. It is a fascinating conversation. Minute by minute, it leads to new questions, at least on my behalf.

And I think about the most recent one on accountability of the President. You know I hate to bring up the sore subject of Ben Rhodes but I don't see any accountability. I mean I see Ben Rhodes on the TV from Laos this week and I, myself, wrote the President a letter asking him to relieve Ben Rhodes for his forays that were made public.

That having been said, I know the 1947 Act doesn't specifically talk about qualifications but you fine gentlemen who have worked in the industry maybe could lead us in the right direction. And I would also say right here that I am not an advocate of Congress meddling too much in the President's business. And I think that regardless of the President's party or who that person is, everybody wants the President to have the tools that he or she needs to complete the mission. But it is apparent, I think, to most people, that this things is pretty broken for whatever reason. And without any congressional oversight, we are completely relying on the executive to make the correct decisions. And once it gets a level or two below him or her, it seems like the rules are being made up as they go for the expedience of whatever at the moment is garnering the attention.

So, with that in mind what should—I looked at Ben Rhodes' qualifications, knowing what he was involved in, the level. This is national security. This is national policy that affects millions of lives and the world and I think that the qualifications for that individual have to be profound and robust in my opinion. I mean I don't have the qualifications to do what some of these folks are doing and I wouldn't deign to think that I do. What should they be and how does that come about?

Anybody.

Ambassador BLOOMFIELD. If I could give a perspective, Congressman Perry. I can't answer about individuals in the current administration but it has been my observation, and I made this in my testimony, that because the agencies in the national security space are so bloated with so many empowered people doing you name it, there are 80 direct reports to the Secretary of State by my count. That is just an unbelievable fact. And I would say OSD and OJCS and, as Congressman Rohrabacher pointed out, the intel community with 800 new billets layered on top of the 16 agencies.

So, that is out there. Now you have the NSC staff which has grown into several hundred. And if you could just imagine, and we all can try to imagine, the President inside the Oval Office saying, ''Who are all these people?'' You are getting huge amounts of paperwork from all of these agencies. Then, you have hundreds of people that you met once, when they came in to say hello and take your picture. I sort of can understand why he would take five people that he trusts and say close the door, we will figure it out. Sort of a treehouse mentality. I don't mean to be——

Mr. PERRY. And I would agree with you. It is just a process problem. My perception in years past is that it was four or five, 10 people that the President trusted and that is who the NSC was now. It is apparent now that that is who the current President trusts and I don't blame him. But who are all these other people and why do we need them? What have they got to do with anything?

What are their responsibilities regarding the national security strategy? Anybody?

Mr. CHOLLET. Sure. And Congressman, I served for a year and a half as the Senior Director for Strategic Planning at the White House. In terms of the creation of the national security strategy of the United States, which happens once every 3 years or so——

Mr. PERRY. But you know what the statute is, don't you?

Mr. CHOLLET. Yes, yes, yes.

Mr. PERRY. So, in 8 years now, we will have it done twice when it is required every single year.

Mr. CHOLLET. Sure. I mean unfortunately, as someone who owned the strategic planning operation or ran it, I would have wanted to see it done more often but it has traditionally been done, going back to when the statute was created, I think twice in an administration. Bush did it twice. I think Clinton did it twice or did it more than twice.

Mr. PERRY. So, do we need a change in the standard since, apparently, we can't abide by the standard? What are the consequences of not abiding by the standard? Poor policy, right? Poor execution.

Mr. CHOLLET. I believe there should be more strategic thinking in the White House. I very much applaud that recommendation in Atlantic Council's Report. As I said, we tried mightily to give our senior policymakers more time to think strategically and get out of the inbox but the press of events has been unrelenting.

And just very quickly, if I could, sir——

Mr. PERRY. So, hold that thought for a minute and then continue it afterward. But do you have a recommendation regarding—to me one of the bigger issues is we have all these new people, all these great minds. We can't even get a national security strategy out. How does the national military strategy follow no national security strategy? How does anybody know what the plan is?

Mr. CHOLLET. I think one of the most important things that a new administration can do is try to get the sequencing right in how they do these strategies because no administration has gotten it right, where you start with the national security strategy, then you do the QDR, then you do the QDDR, and then you do all the other sort of agency-level strategies. And unfortunately, because of different oversight committees, different processes in the different departments, those are not well-aligned and it doesn't make much sense. I concede that.

Can I just say very briefly, not to get into individuals but I should, Ben Rhodes is a friend and colleague. I worked with him very closely during my time in the administration. He is one of the most talented people I have worked with in Washington. I have worked here for 20 years with a lot of talented people.

That said, both at DoD, State, and at the NSC, there a lot of folks that I worked with who were the best in the business and there are a lot of folks I worked with or some, I should say, that I worked with and I wondered how they got there.

This goes back to a question that I was given earlier that I didn't get a chance to answer which was there isn't really any quality training done really in any of the positions in the national security field. Basically, once you get out of school or if you are in the career foreign service or in the military you get a chance to do a stint at NDU, I think that is something we should take very seriously. I believe in past authorization bills from the State Department, that issue has been looked at, sort of career professional training but to ensure that we do have a higher standard in all of our agencies for senior officials.

Mr. PERRY. Let me just conclude with this, Mr. Chairman. Regardless of Ben Rhodes' talents, and I acknowledge he seems like a very talented individual by what I have read and what I have seen, nothing, nothing at all regarding his talent explains or justifies deceiving the American people outwardly, regardless of the policy outcome.

The ends do not justify the means and I find it reprehensible, unacceptable, and I think it is a black mark on the administration and on American policy and that is my opinion.

But with that, I yield back.

Mr. ROHRABACHER. Thank you. He ended it on a different kind of note. That is fine.

But Ms. Bass, you may begin it on any kind of note that you would like.

Ms. BASS. Well, thanks for letting us know how you really feel.

Thank you very much for your testimony. I think this has been a very, very, very interesting discussion. And I just wanted to ask a few questions.

One, as I listen to the three of you, and I want you to tell me whether I am right or wrong, there are things that need to be improved in the NSC but I don't think I heard any of you say that we are in some kind of crisis and that there is something terribly wrong.

I guess listening whether we should increase or decrease the staff, what worries me about that is that it seems rather mechanical and I can absolutely appreciate what you were saying Mr. Chollet, if I am pronouncing your name correctly, about how things have changed so much, especially from Bloomfield, you know what you were saying.

Mr. Chollet, you mentioned climate change and I was wondering how—cybersecurity I certainly understand but I was wondering if you could give me an example of how climate change fits in there.

But if each of you could respond to: We are not in a crisis, there are things that could be improved, but there is no great disaster happening. Am I correct in what I hear?

Mr. CHOLLET. I will take the first shot, if I could.

Ms. BASS. Okay.

Mr. CHOLLET. I agree with you. I don't think it is a crisis but I think it is legitimate and good that this committee, the Congress, the strategic community, those of us on the outside now are looking into this issue because we have an opportunity here coming up with a new President taking office to reform the NSC, to try to right-size it, to try to ensure that we are getting the most we can out of it, and to help the incoming administration think about these important issues that they are going to be inheriting because the NSC is very malleable.

The only thing in statute is the members of the actual NSC, the senior level members, and establishing the Executive Secretary. Everything else, the President can do things totally differently. And so climate change is a perfect example where that is an issue that didn't exist much 25 years ago and now, of course, it has been a major issue internationally and a major priority for this administration. So, although it is an issue set that doesn't solely reside in the NSC because there are other agencies within the Executive Office of the President that deal with the various issue of climate change, clearly, the effort of the United States Government to try to get at this issue, both in terms of how we behave here at home but also how we negotiate abroad is something the NSC has had to follow as the President has been engaging in international diplomacy on this issue.

Ms. BASS. Oh, so it is because he has been engaging in international diplomacy that he has——

Mr. CHOLLET. Both. I mean it is a priority. This is one of the greatest international——

Ms. BASS. Right. I just didn't see. I mean believe me, I understand the significance of climate change. I just didn't see its relation here.

Ambassador BLOOMFIELD. Can I just take a moment?

Congresswoman Bass, I will be the one that says crisis is too strong a word but the bus only shows up every 4 years before an election when you can think a little bit out of the in-basket and say what should we be fixing.

I think we have something verging on a crisis in our national security community——

Ms. BASS. Okay——

Ambassador BLOOMFIELD [continuing]. And it is not personal to President Obama or any of the members of his team who have been named today. It is broader than that and it is more historic.

There is a foreign diplomat in Asia who made a comment a few years ago that is true. He said when he deals with other governments, they take 20 percent of the time figuring out their policy and 80 percent implementing it.

Ms. BASS. Oh.

Ambassador BLOOMFIELD. But in Washington it is reversed.

Ms. BASS. Yes.

Ambassador BLOOMFIELD. I have spent much of my life watching the internecine battles between people trying to hang onto their authority, their issue. I will give you one example. My old bureau, the Political Military Bureau, went into Libya, after Ghadafi was taken down, to look for loose weapons and shoulder-fired missiles and arms with U.N. folks.

Then came Syria. And I remember Congressman Royce held a hearing on Syrian chemical weapons. But because chemical weapons are WMDs, that is a different bureau. We had teams on the ground, operational, with communications, ready to go, but a different bureau said no, that is my turf. And that is just one of a thousand, I used the term "thousand bowls of rice" in my testimony and I see that. And I think we need to address it.

Ms. BASS. Okay.

Ambassador MILLER. Very quickly, Ms. Bass, I think crisis is the wrong term but it is close. Crises today seem to be defined by what is on the right-hand column of The Washington Post front page, whatever. We are in a significant crisis in terms of the stature of the United States in the world, full stop. If you are traveling out there, you are going to get an earful. If you are an old Ambassador, you are used to being criticized. But it is getting worse and we need to step back and take a serious look about how our country is developing international strategy and as Linc was saying, then, how we implement.

Much of our report focuses on the fact that there may have been reasonable strategic decisions made but the implementation was poor enough to jeopardize the outcome and I think that is a very serious issue.

And one last observation and that is, one of the things that you are observing is the White House is trying to solve many, many, many problems. There is not a staff at the White House of the size to solve all the problems that really fall under the jurisdiction of cabinet secretaries and agency heads.

And so I think one of the things that we need to look at is the proper use of the cabinet officials and the agency heads to say the President cares a great deal about X and he wants you, Madam Secretary, to go do that, not to add another layer of people at the White House.

Thank you.

Ms. BASS. Thank you.

Mr. ROHRABACHER. Mr. DeSantis.

Mr. DeSANTIS. Thank you, Mr. Chairman.

So, I think that there are probably too many people in the NSC. I think there are too many people in a lot of parts of government but to me, it is the authority that they are exercising that is more important than the sheer numbers. In other words, if I had to choose between a bloated staff that was basically serving the core advisory function versus a leaner staff that was actually usurping the authorities of the secretaries, I would choose the former. Are most of you in agreement with that? I know Ambassador Bloomfield.

And part of the reason is I think when you have the model gravitating toward where is more policy being implemented by the NSC, it really detracts from the accountability that the American people have.

I mean, for example, Ambassador Bloomfield, I saw you served in different positions. You had to get confirmed by the Senate for those positions.

Ambassador BLOOMFIELD. Yes.

Mr. DeSANTIS. And those were Deputy Assistant posts in the State Department?

Ambassador BLOOMFIELD. Assistant Secretary and above.

Mr. DeSANTIS. Right. At the NSC, for example, we mentioned Ben Rhodes as the Deputy. He did not have to get confirmed by the Senate, correct? And he has been described as the most influential voice shaping U.S. foreign policy, other than President Obama, himself.

And so I think that somebody who is really wielding that much influence in our affairs of State should at least have to sit and get Senate confirmation. And if Rhodes is an advisor to the President and that is what he is doing, fine. But if he is implementing policy, if he is crafting things with the Iran deal, with Cuba, that becomes much different. And Ben Rhodes, and I appreciate your comments about him, obviously, we have had disagreements with him because of how the Iran deal has been handled. We wanted to invite him to testify but he is a member of the staff and so he doesn't come.

He would not have been able to be confirmed to be Secretary of State or Secretary of Defense. I mean that is just the reality of the situation.

So, you are putting people who are implementing policy without having the check of Senate confirmation. And again, if there are White House advisors, I don't want us dragging in an actual counselor to the President. I think that there are absolutely legitimate separation of powers concerns there.

But then you also have this idea of putting the power in the hands of the NSC staff; then, you don't have congressional oversight, which is what we need to do.

Secretary Kerry has to come here because Congress controls the budget. Secretary of Defense has to come here and they have to answer questions about how the policy is being conducted. That is good for Congress but it is also good for the American people to be able to see what is going on.

As I mentioned, we wanted to figure out how this Iran deal happened. We invited Ben Rhodes and he declined to come. And I think his position, as it should be, I think that would be legitimate but I think he was exercising authority that went beyond that.

And then I guess the final thing that I think about when you have people on the NSC staff getting involved with military commanders in the field, totally going outside the normal chain of command. If we had military commanders that bucked the chain of command, they would never be able to get away with that. I mean that would be a cardinal sin to do it. And so we have a very clear chain of command. When you have a combatant commander they are reporting up to the Secretary of Defense and then to the President. It should be that we can't have the NSC staff just basically going around the chain of command.

Ambassador Miller, you wanted to——

Ambassador MILLER. Yes, just very quickly on that. At least one of our intelligence agencies has handled the communications issue by basically saying no calls to staff in the field from the White House will be answered, full stop. Those calls will be referred to a headquarters across the river and we will worry about responding to staff.

We got, in our interviews, we got really, really tough commentary from the military. You all know General Mattis and a wonderful group, virtually all from the Naval Service, who felt very strongly about that.

One other, just one comment on confirmation. I, obviously, went through the confirmation process in the ambassadorial assignments and I found it very valuable. I learned a lot. An Ambassador represents not just the President but the country. So, I think a dialogue with the Congress is actually very helpful.

And when I was at the NSC, I was immensely comfortable coming up here to discuss issues where I knew members had concerns and nobody had to ask me to testify. I was happy to come up and talk. And I think that the end of my testimony speaks to that and that is, you can't legislate trust. You can't change organizations to create trust. You have to just begin to work with each other to the point that you say yes, these are all pretty bright guys and they all care about the country. And I hope that is where we might begin to move here.

I am sorry I took so long with that.

Mr. DeSANTIS. That is okay. My time has expired but I appreciate all of you guys coming and testifying. And I think that there is probably a consensus that this is not operating the precise way it was envisioned and we would like to see some changes with the next administration.

I yield back.

Chairman ROYCE [presiding]. Thank you, Mr. DeSantis.

Mr. Gerry Connolly of Virginia.

Mr. CONNOLLY. Thank you, Mr. Chairman.

I will inform my friend from Florida I don't know that we all agree. I certainly don't agree with his analysis in terms of the prescription.

Frankly, how Congress is approaching this through the Armed Services Committee, not through the Foreign Affairs or Foreign Relations Committees, reminds me of H. L. Mencken. You know for every human problem, there is a solution. There is a solution; simple, neat, and wrong.

I mean I heard my friend Mr. Perry talk about maybe that old system of 10 advisors is what we ought to go back to. Well, I mean, if you are worried about unwieldy bureaucracies in the White House, let us go back to Lincoln's model. He had two secretaries. Would that work? That would certainly not be unwieldy. I don't know that it would. And he had to deal with a Civil War. So, what is wrong with that? It is a big, difficult, complex world.

Ambassador Miller, you mentioned one of the prescriptions was, make the State Department work. I thought that was a profound statement.

Ambassador MILLER. Yes.

Mr. CONNOLLY. One of the reasons a President turns to a group of advisors is because the bureaucracy doesn't work for them.

Ambassador MILLER. I know.

Mr. CONNOLLY. Thank God there were low-level people telling the President a different thing than Curtis LeMay during the Cuban Missile Crisis. If we had followed the chain of command strictly, rigidly, after all, he has the stars, he has been confirmed, we would have gone to World War III. Curtis LeMay wanted to bomb Cuba, even though he didn't even know that in fact some of the missiles in fact had already been nuclear tipped and were acclimated. Thank God there were other voices than the chain of command.

There are times the bureaucracy, and I don't mean that in any pejorative way, produces great statesmen and stateswomen. And thank God it does. The very best rises to the top. There are other times that is not so true. And the President has to rely on a group of younger people to give him some advice and, soon, maybe her.

And so it seems to me, a little thing up here, Congress doesn't do nuance. And so if you look at the legislation, what does it do? What is our fix for this vague problem, that it is too big? Well, I don't know. What would make you happy? What would be the ideal Goldilocks solution for the NSC size?

And by the way, why have we chosen the NSC? Mr. Chollet, you mentioned, would you remind us how big the staff of the Joint Chiefs of Staff at the Pentagon is?

Mr. CHOLLET. It is roughly seven times larger than the current NSC.

Mr. CONNOLLY. Seven times and no one is talking about that. Is that a problem? When you were in the White House, was that ever a problem?

Mr. CHOLLET. They had more charts than we did.

Mr. CONNOLLY. Was there ever confusion as to who was speaking for whom?

Mr. CHOLLET. No.

Mr. CONNOLLY. Well, I just I think we need to tread lightly. I don't think that the legislation only ought to have the imprint of the Armed Services Committee. I think it needs some foreign policy overlay and I think we need to understand what problem it is that we are fixing.

It may be that it is too big and too unwieldy and not coordinated and some people overstep their lines. Of course that is going to happen but does that merit draconian legislation that says you can only have 100?

How many are on the NSC staff now, Mr. Chollet?

Mr. CHOLLET. It is about 190 policy staff.

Mr. CONNOLLY. Okay, so we are roughly cutting it in half. And if you want to go above that, as the chairman indicated, NSC gets confirmed.

Now, this is why I cited Mencken. Let us assume for a minute, stipulate there is a problem and that is the problem. The solution guarantees all the things you don't like, guarantees institutional friction until the cows come home because now I am your equal. I am confirmed, too. And I got actually official status to get you in a lot of trouble over there at the State Department or the Pentagon because I am confirmed like you are. And I am not sure that is the solution.

You know if there was someone who understood that, it was the guy who probably started all this problem, Henry Kissinger. Because when he finally got the confirmable job, he kept the NSC job, too, because he didn't want that tension. And that is an interesting model for us to contemplate.

At any rate, I am sorry, but the chairman has graciously said I could have an extra minute or two to compensate for Mr. Rohrabacher. So, this is your comment.

Ambassador BLOOMFIELD. Could I just put another idea before you? And this is in the spirit of nonpartisanship. Every time there is an election, the winning team has a plum book and gives away political appointments. I have been in an political appointed position for five administrations. We have watched, over the decades, as lower and lower levels of the bureaucracy are awarded to political appointees, people who are loyal, who were helpful on a campaign, that sort of thing, who may have been contributors. And I think that we could look at that issue and ask, because as Mr. Perry brought up the question of qualifications, it may be there are just too many jobs in the foreign policy bureaucracy being awarded to people who had talents in the political arena but really didn't have background or any seasoning in the foreign policy and national security arena. And that is something that would be a bipartisan endeavor. So, I thought I would put that out there as part of the record of the hearing.

Ambassador MILLER. Mr. Connolly, I think it is time for a nuanced look at the State Department.

Mr. CONNOLLY. And I reiterate, that is not us.

Ambassador MILLER. Yes, but somebody up here has to have a nuanced approach to the State Department. It is an institution. And I will say this again, every foreign service officer that came out of the White House who worked for me, they were superb. You put them back in the State Department and they are put back into a structure that doesn't function well.

The cure, if you will, is complex. It is a problem that has grown over many years. And I would hope that a group of staff people up here could begin under your direction to say what all might we consider as a new administration arrives to make the Department work better. If it doesn't, you are not going to solve whatever NSC problem you think you are facing.

Mr. CHOLLET. Just one brief comment. And I think this is why this hearing is so important because it creates the space for a new administration to perhaps make some change.

I can speak personally from the transition from Bush to Obama, where we also came in with some big ideas about how the NSC should work better; the NSC was way too big under President Bush and we would make it slimmer and hold the agencies accountable. But then once in office, there was also an imperative don't screw up. Don't change things for the sake of changing things before you actually know what you are doing, particularly when we are a nation at war.

And this gets back to holding the President accountable. We want and the President should be held accountable. The President is the one who got elected. But at the same time, in order help the President make the system work as best as she or he can, there also needs to be a sense that there is space that should be allowed to make those important decisions and, perhaps, absorb some risk because that is part of the issue—the President's national security advisors don't want to take the risk. If I cut the staff too much and take away that oversight and that accountability that I am trying achieve here to serve the President, then we are going to get burned on the other end if something goes wrong.

Mr. CONNOLLY. Mr. Chairman, I just want to thank you for the indulgence and I think our witnesses were great. And I really think this is a great contribution to a very important subject and I would hope that our committee will weigh in and not cede this entirely to the Armed Services Committee because I think it is just too important.

And again, I thank you so much for holding this hearing.

Chairman ROYCE. Well, I thank you, Mr. Connolly. And I do think we may have stretched a point with Mr. Bloomfield's opinions on the bureaucracy at the size of the Pentagon. Based on his writings, I suspect he is every bit as much concerned with the size of the bureaucracy there as he is with the size of the NSC.

I would just make a point that there seems to be no disagreement among those that have worked at the NSC that the current size increases dysfunction. There does seem to be that conclusion. Reducing its size can only help and it is good that the administration is moving in that direction.

I want to also express my appreciation for the time of our witnesses today. This has been, I think, as I share Mr. Connolly's view, that this should be the purview of this committee. This has been a very informative hearing. We have had good participation today from the members.

As Ambassador Miller said, the NSC is the heart of the foreign policy machine. And I took that analogy to heart but your other point is that there can be heart failure and then we have a massive problem. And you know I think the next administration's goal should be getting back to the core function of the NSC and that is coordinating policy, coordinating policy where the diplomats are doing the diplomacy and the military has oversight over the military and the NSC can give the President the policy options that it is intended to. And if not, then Congress has to step in and that is especially true when it comes to accountability. That is our role.

And I thank our witnesses again. And, Mr. Connolly, thank you. We stand adjourned.

[Whereupon, at 11:59 a.m., the committee was adjourned.]

APPENDIX

Material Submitted for the Record

FULL COMMITTEE HEARING NOTICE
COMMITTEE ON FOREIGN AFFAIRS
U.S. HOUSE OF REPRESENTATIVES
WASHINGTON, DC 20515-6128

Edward R. Royce (R-CA), Chairman

September 8, 2016

TO: MEMBERS OF THE COMMITTEE ON FOREIGN AFFAIRS

You are respectfully requested to attend an OPEN hearing of the Committee on Foreign Affairs, to be held in Room 2172 of the Rayburn House Office Building (and available live on the Committee website at http://www.ForeignAffairs.house.gov):

DATE: Thursday, September 8, 2016

TIME: 10:00 a.m.

SUBJECT: Reforming the National Security Council: Efficiency and Accountability

WITNESSES: The Honorable David C. Miller, Jr.
                   Non-Resident Senior Fellow
                   The Atlantic Council
                   (Former Special Assistant to the President, National Security Council)

                   The Honorable Lincoln P. Bloomfield, Jr.
                   Chairman of the Board
                   The Stimson Center
                   (Former Assistant Secretary for Political Military Affairs, U.S. Department of State)

                   The Honorable Derek Chollet
                   Counselor and Senior Advisor for Security and Defense Policy
                   The German Marshall Fund of the United States
                   (Former Assistant Secretary for International Security Affairs, U.S. Department of Defense)

By Direction of the Chairman

The Committee on Foreign Affairs seeks to make its facilities accessible to persons with disabilities. If you are in need of special accommodations, please call 202/225-5021 at least four business days in advance of the event, whenever practicable. Questions with regard to special accommodations in general (including availability of Committee materials in alternative formats and assistive listening devices) may be directed to the Committee.

COMMITTEE ON FOREIGN AFFAIRS
MINUTES OF FULL COMMITTEE HEARING

Day __*Thursday*__ Date _____*9/8/2016*_____ Room _____*2172*_____

Starting Time _____*10:10*_____ Ending Time _____*12:00*_____

Recesses | *0* | (____to____) (____to____) (____to____) (____to____) (____to____) (____to____)

Presiding Member(s)
Chairman Edward R. Royce, Rep. Dana Rohrabacher

Check all of the following that apply:

Open Session ☑   Electronically Recorded (taped) ☑
Executive (closed) Session ☐   Stenographic Record ☑
Televised ☑

TITLE OF HEARING:

Reforming the National Security Council: Efficiency and Accountability

COMMITTEE MEMBERS PRESENT:

See attached.

NON-COMMITTEE MEMBERS PRESENT:

none

HEARING WITNESSES: Same as meeting notice attached? Yes ☑ No ☐
(If "no", please list below and include title, agency, department, or organization.)

STATEMENTS FOR THE RECORD: *(List any statements submitted for the record.)*

SFR - Rep. Gerald Connolly
IFR - Ambassador David Miller
IFR - Ambassador Lincoln Bloomfield

TIME SCHEDULED TO RECONVENE _____
or
TIME ADJOURNED *12:00*

_____
Full Committee Hearing Coordinator

HOUSE COMMITTEE ON FOREIGN AFFAIRS
FULL COMMITTEE HEARING

PRESENT	MEMBER	PRESENT	MEMBER
X	Edward R. Royce, CA	X	Eliot L. Engel, NY
X	Christopher H. Smith, NJ	X	Brad Sherman, CA
X	Ileana Ros-Lehtinen, FL		Gregory W. Meeks, NY
X	Dana Rohrabacher, CA	X	Albio Sires, NJ
	Steve Chabot, OH	X	Gerald E. Connolly, VA
X	Joe Wilson, SC	X	Theodore E. Deutch, FL
	Michael T. McCaul, TX		Brian Higgins, NY
	Ted Poe, TX	X	Karen Bass, CA
X	Matt Salmon, AZ	X	William Keating, MA
	Darrell Issa, CA	X	David Cicilline, RI
	Tom Marino, PA		Alan Grayson, FL
X	Jeff Duncan, SC	X	Ami Bera, CA
X	Mo Brooks, AL	X	Alan S. Lowenthal, CA
	Paul Cook, CA	X	Grace Meng, NY
	Randy Weber, TX	X	Lois Frankel, FL
X	Scott Perry, PA	X	Tulsi Gabbard, HI
X	Ron DeSantis, FL	X	Joaquin Castro, TX
	Mark Meadows, NC		Robin Kelly, IL
X	Ted Yoho, FL		Brendan Boyle, PA
	Curt Clawson, FL		
	Scott DesJarlais, TN		
X	Reid Ribble, WI		
	Dave Trott, MI		
X	Lee Zeldin, NY		
X	Dan Donovan, NY		

Statement for the Record
Submitted by Mr. Connolly of Virginia

The National Security Council (NSC) was established by the 1947 National Security Act (P.L. 80-253). The founding legislation for the NSC was referred to the Committee on Oversight and Government Reform in the House, and the Armed Services Committee in the Senate. However, the history of the NSC is replete with instances in which the activities of the NSC have ventured into the jurisdiction of the House Foreign Affairs Committee, and we should welcome a thoughtful discussion on proposals to reform its underlying statute, which has not changed drastically for more than 60 years.

The prescriptions for NSC reform most recently advanced in the Senate and House versions of the National Defense Authorization Act for FY2017 are caps on the number of NSC staff. The House would limit the NSC staff to 100 and require Senate confirmation of the National Security Advisor if the staff size exceeds the limit. The Senate would provide a simple cap of 150 personnel, including detailees.

To paraphrase H.L. Mencken, for every complex human problem, there is a solution that is simple, neat, and wrong. These caps on staff size are arbitrary and they infringe on a long-established practice of allowing the Executive Office of the President to organize its staff. This is micromanagement for the purposes of preventing micromanagement.

There is no doubt we should be sympathetic to claims from former Secretaries of Defense and State regarding micromanagement and competing mandates with the NSC. The NSC has a long history, for better or for worse, of micromanagement and interference with other agencies. The Iran-Contra affair and National Security Advisor Henry Kissinger surreptitiously altering U.S. China policy come to mind.

However, to require Senate confirmation of the NSA in order to protect the institutional prerogative of cabinet-level agencies actually aggravates the problem. This proposal would codify the agency conflict with the NSC and establish a competing and co-equal policymaking apparatus in direct competition with the very departments we are trying to help, the Department of Defense and the Department of State.

While a conspiracy by the White House to steal the policy prerogatives of executive branch agencies is one possible explanation for NSC staff expansion, it is far more likely that the growth of an entity tasked with interagency coordination is due to the vacuum created by deficient or nonexistent interagency mechanisms in other agencies. The NSC is a relatively small cohort within the vast machinery of the U.S. diplomatic, homeland security, and defense operations, and an examination of the NSC and any deficiencies found therein would likely constitute an indictment that extends beyond the Council and its staff. Attempts to reform the NSC should not be reduced to a simple number. The NSC is tasked with interagency coordination, and an effort to reform any such coordinating entity should take a whole of government approach.

Reform efforts should also ensure that the NSC's underlying statue imbues the Council and its staff with the mission, passion, and metrics necessary for a successful organization. While the substance of foreign policy is quick to garner the attention of Congress, the process by which it is coordinated and implemented is often overlooked. We must ensure that both the NSC and the agencies with which it interfaces are equipped with the mandates, authorities, and resources necessary to fulfill their mission. This is a constructive approach to improving government. Simple caps on staff size are not.

MATERIAL SUBMITTED FOR THE RECORD BY THE HONORABLE DAVID C. MILLER, JR.,
NON-RESIDENT SENIOR FELLOW, THE ATLANTIC COUNCIL (FORMER SPECIAL ASSIST-
ANT TO THE PRESIDENT, NATIONAL SECURITY COUNCIL)

Atlantic Council

The National Security Council Reform Project

A FOUNDATIONAL PROPOSAL FOR THE NEXT ADMINISTRATION

Chester A. Crocker • Daniel Levin
David C. Miller, Jr. • Thomas R. Pickering

FOREWORD BY BRENT SCOWCROFT

JASON T. KIRBY, CHIEF OF STAFF

The National Security Council Reform Project

A FOUNDATIONAL PROPOSAL
FOR THE NEXT ADMINISTRATION

Chester A. Crocker
Daniel Levin
David C. Miller, Jr.
Thomas R. Pickering

With Foreword by Brent Scowcroft

Jason T. Kirby, Chief of Staff

ISBN: 978-1-61977-481-0

Publication design: April Brady; Cover photo credit: twak, altered and licensed under Creative Commons.

June 2016

"During the Cold War, we were facing nuclear war if we screwed up. That was an incentive to get it right, to stay ahead of developments. Today, we have no strategy that covers the entire world – the changes that are coming. And there's a lot of change going. For 500 years, we lived under Westphalian nation-state systems. But globalization has eroded borders. For the first time this world's people are politicized, interconnected by technology. The nature of power is changing. The nature of international cooperation is changing. The nature of conflict is changing. We're not evolving well to adapt. This world is not as dangerous as that during the Cold War, but it is much more complicated."

—Lieutenant General Brent Scowcroft, USAF (Ret.)
9th and 17th United States Assistant to the President for National Security Affairs

TABLE OF CONTENTS

FOREWORD

BRENT SCOWCROFT

Dear Colleague,

There follows a report on the organization and performance of the National Security Council system, a subject to which I have given a good deal of thought over many years. It broadly reflects my views and those of others that have served in both Republican and Democratic administrations. Those who were interviewed or participated in seminars in the preparation of this report include more than sixty senior foreign policy, defense, and intelligence leaders. They include three- and four-star military commanders, secretaries of state and defense and other cabinet officers, senior intelligence officials, and lawyers who held senior positions at the White House and the Department of Justice.

They share a deeply held, bipartisan concern that our country has too often suffered from strategic confusion with many unintended consequences due to a failure to think two or three steps ahead. They also frequently cite the same examples of poor execution of policies that might have enjoyed much greater success if they had been well managed.

The Atlantic Council and the authors of this study believe that a well-run National Security Council system is the key to strategic coherence and thoughtful execution of national policy. Thus this report.

This report focuses on three key observations that surfaced during these interviews. First, the size of the NSC staff has increased to numbers never seen in the first five decades after it was created in 1947. This development has had major consequences for the functioning of the interagency NSC process. Second, the NSC has increasingly moved away from its traditional principal role of coordinating inputs and advice from the relevant executive branch departments and agencies to a role of active involvement in the daily management of foreign policy. And finally, not only has the staff grown dramatically in number, but criteria for selection has allowed for more junior personnel with limited expertise and a high turnover rate.

There is a great deal written about these observations in the report that follows. The report is organized into two documents of increasing size and granularity—from an executive summary to a much longer, detailed discussion of the issues raised in the interviews.

It is our hope that an incoming administration will read this report carefully. There is much to be learned from history. Reforming the size, mission, and staffing of the NSC can bring a return to models that have succeeded over many decades. Good structure does not guarantee success, but bad structure almost always overcomes good people and leads to poor results.

Brent Scowcroft

Lieutenant General Brent Scowcroft, USAF (Ret.)
Assistant to the President for National Security Affairs
November 3, 1975–January 20, 1977
January 20, 1989–January 20, 1993

WASHINGTON, D.C.

EXECUTIVE SUMMARY

There is a growing consensus that the United States has made serious mistakes in foreign and defense policy over the past two decades. These problems can be observed in the administrations of both political parties. They are rooted both in a failure to define clearly our international strategic objectives and in the poor execution of what we have pursued. These issues have been aggravated by a failure to anticipate both the direct impact and the unintended consequences of our actions. This inability to effectively execute foreign policy and manage military force projection has eroded public confidence in our government and the perception of American leadership globally.

This foundational report serves as a point of departure for the next administration. It contains the essential elements for building the most effective national security structure in the small window between today and the first hundred days of the next administration. The perceived simplicity of these foundational recommendations has eluded many of the preceding administrations that have tried to implement some of the elements that you will read here.

Over the past two years, this document's authors—**Ambassadors Chester Crocker, David Miller, and Thomas Pickering; the Honorable Daniel Levin; and Chief of Staff, Colonel (sel.) Jason Kirby**—personally conducted over sixty interviews with senior foreign policy, military, and intelligence officials. These officials included seven former national security advisors (NSAs),[1] eight cabinet members and deputies, and seven three- and four-star flag officers. It is our conclusion that an important contributing factor to the problems stated above has been the structural and personnel failures at the National Security Council (NSC) in the management of foreign, defense, intelligence, and legal policy. An incoming president has much to be gained by establishing an effective NSC and much to lose if the NSC is poorly structured from the beginning.

We believe an incoming president has seven fundamental decisions to make regarding the organization, staffing, and management of the National Security Council:

1. Focus the National Security Council Mission

2. Define the National Security Advisor's Role

3. Reduce and Restrict the Size of the NSC Staff

4. Designate a Strategic Planning Staff

5. Use Interagency Teams and Task Forces

6. Coordinate Legal Advice

7. Prepare for the Transition Now

As members of most prior administrations have learned, these decisions greatly influence the success or failure of the White House's foreign and defense policy management. It is understood that an incoming president will define the NSC structure that he or she wants, but the president should be aware that these choices have direct consequences for the success or failure of the policy process. Our recommendations for how these decisions should be made are based on our own experience as well as the many interviews we conducted.

SEVEN KEY RECOMMENDATIONS

Focus the National Security Council Mission. Properly defining the mission of the NSC staff is the most important decision as it largely drives the other matters discussed below. The mission of the NSC is to coordinate the development of policy options for the president using the most effective application of US diplomatic, economic, military, and intelligence resources. In doing so, the NSC presents, and seeks to incorporate and harmonize, the NSC principals' recommended policy positions. The NSC staff ensures the president's policy decisions are properly executed by integrating, supporting, and tracking—and not themselves executing, with few, if any, exceptions—the implementation of foreign and defense policy by the departments and agencies. That is, the NSC must be a coordinating "honest broker," not a miniature and operational foreign policy establishment housed

---

[1] In this report, the term NSA refers to the role of national security advisor, not the National Security Agency.

within the White House. This honest broker role builds trust and confidence—straightforward, perceptive, and wise recommendations build success.

Define the National Security Advisor's Role. The selection of the national security advisor is critically important. It is arguably the most important appointment a president will make without the advice and consent of the Senate. Experienced advisors can make many structures work; inexperienced individuals can cause any structure or plan to fail. In addition to extensive foreign and security policy expertise, chief among the desired qualifications are government management experience, and the ability (and desire) to act as honest broker. This most often takes the form of seeking out and promoting multiple viewpoints for the benefit of the president's decision-making. Compatibility with the president and his or her national security team is essential. The quality of the NSC staff also flows from the selection of a competent advisor. To staff the NSC, successful national security advisors recruited outstanding foreign and security policy professionals who wanted to work with and learn from them.

Reduce and Restrict the Size of the NSC Staff. The largest professional staff recommended by any former official was two hundred, with most counseling seventy-five to a hundred. Given the expanding number of issues and crises that recent administrations have faced in the twenty-first century, limiting the NSC staff size to **100 to 150 professionals** is appropriate. The size of the NSC professional staff helps determine how a president will manage policy and supervise execution.

A staff of hundreds sends a clear message that the president largely intends to try operating foreign policy and force projection within his or her own White House staff. A smaller staff almost always means the president will rely more on the NSC principals, and the departments and agencies they lead, and leave the NSC staff to its traditional role of interagency coordination, support, and integration. The departments and agencies are then sized and funded to execute day-to-day management of diplomatic and military policy, something they have been tasked with and have executed for decades. A large size contributes to the distrust observed between the NSC staff and the career employees of the departments, agencies, and the uniformed services, and as the NSC's role shifts from supporting and integrating to directing it begins to duplicate agency roles that are almost always beyond its capacity to carry out effectively. A larger staff can also isolate the president and senior staff because it leads to conflict with cabinet officers themselves. When staff size balloons, instead of synchronizing the departments and agencies, the staff instead engenders and enables debilitating interagency battles and poor judgment over time. Finally, size exacerbates problems

with largely uncontrolled, uncoordinated, and often unknown communication from all levels of the NSC staff to departments and agencies as well as foreign missions in Washington and American embassies.

Designate a Strategic Planning Staff. Weakness in long-term strategic planning for foreign and defense policy has been observed consistently during a number of past administrations. There is a Gresham's Law at work in which daily needs drive out longer-term strategic thinking and planning, just as operational control drives out the capacity and time to formulate clear and useful policy options. While the departments and agencies contain strategic planning functions (for example, the policy planning staff at the Department of State and strategy staff at the Office of the Secretary of Defense), there is no set structure within the NSC to bring both lessons learned and strategic planning functions together on a regular and continuing basis in response to presidential requests and national needs. An effective foreign policy will, of course, be guided by smart strategy, but it must adapt the ways, means, and, when necessary, ends of that strategy to account for changed circumstances—including opportunities.

The allocation of roles and staff between strategic planning and daily integration functions should be clarified, perhaps by creating a deputy assistant to the president and a small office of five professionals dedicated to considering and integrating options before advising the president on the strategic recommendations of the NSC staff and the various departments and agencies on a regular basis. This deputy assistant would help the president and national security principals develop and disseminate a strategic overview or vision on key issues. This president's own strategic vision would provide a much-needed centerpiece and guide policy and strategy development. If this is not done, the relentless pressure of day-to-day management will continue to drive out long-run thinking and planning, leaving daily decisions to be made based on tactical reflexes without the benefit of a longer-run framework into which decisions should fit. It will eschew the forward vision of chess for the near focus of checkers.

Use Interagency Teams and Task Forces. The appointment of special envoys, representatives, coordinators, ambassadors, czars, and administrators to solve unusually vexing or pressing problems has proliferated under a variety of novel legal structures—and has frequently confused existing authorities and at times has been inadequately supported by the NSA and NSC staff. This practice should be curtailed to those few issues demanding a close relationship to the president and in which the president has a pressing strategic interest. Some serious issues facing the country require the active involvement of a number of departments and agencies over time—sometimes over the life of several administrations. A key to their success is having the NSA appoint as a chair a senior officer from a lead department, closely supported by an NSC special assistant. It has been noted by prior participants in these activities that, given the need for funding, the Office of Management and Budget should be an active member of the strategy development and implementation process. The US response to the Kosovo War (1998–1999) and Plan Colombia (formulated 1998–1999) are notable successes that were chaired by senior officials from the NSC and/or key departments with effective support from the NSC and the related departments and agencies.

Coordinate Legal Advice. The post-9/11 legal environment was understandably one of confusion; decisions were made in a time of crisis, when speed of movement and legal flexibility were paramount. That said, a perception of "lawyer shopping" appears to have led to decisions reached and actions authorized without all of the affected department and agency senior lawyers having access to, and thereby a voice in, the decision-making process. The result has been public distrust and skepticism of the legal decision-making process. The White House legal staff supporting the NSC staff should be highly experienced and lean, tasked with coordinating legal advice while working with the Department of Justice's Office of Legal Counsel and department and agency legal offices. The president should issue a national security directive ensuring that all relevant legal offices throughout the executive branch are transparently included in legal discussions and decisions, and that the process is transparent to the public when appropriate.

Prepare for the Transition Now. The National Security Council's important role requires a transition that assures seamless oversight of our nation's interests and security. The NSC staff is the president's personal foreign policy staff and, as such, all the documents generated over a president's term are properly removed before the transition and sent to a presidential library. In addition, almost all of the personnel are replaced on the day of the transition. Given the NSC's unprecedented role and capacity, a phased personnel transition as well as the retention of some director-level personnel is essential. During the transition period a process of phased personnel replacement, full briefings for incoming staff, and retention of all key documents should be assured. Lead departments and agencies (also undergoing transitions) should plan to play an important role in assuring a smooth transition, watching over breaking developments and knowing the status of NSC-led activities. This transition will be unprecedented due to the volume of key issues being managed by the national security staff. A carefully developed transition leveraging an experienced cadre of leaders will be essential for success.

The 2017 transition teams need to recognize the unusually large number of foreign policy initiatives led by the National Security Council in recent years. The NSC must ensure that the records and history of these activities are not lost in a transition that may require a more comprehensive retention of records and longer transition period for personnel than observed in previous transitions.

[NOTE: The entire report is not reprinted here but may be found on the Internet at: http://docs.house.gov/Committee/Calendar/ByEvent.aspx?EventID=105276]

MATERIAL SUBMITTED FOR THE RECORD BY THE HONORABLE LINCOLN P. BLOOMFIELD, JR., CHAIRMAN OF THE BOARD, THE STIMSON CENTER (FORMER ASSISTANT SECRETARY FOR POLITICAL MILITARY AFFAIRS, U.S. DEPARTMENT OF STATE)

The Next U.S. President's Unspoken Challenge: Management

By Lincoln P. Bloomfield, Jr. *The author is chairman of the non-partisan Stimson Center. He held policy positions in the State Department, the Department of Defense, and the White House during five prior administrations.*

September 2, 2016 - 2:02 pm

In this political season, news reporting and commentary have touched on many issues expected to influence voters. But regardless of who takes the oath of office next January, America's 45th president will find that success rests on a very few basic, but profoundly important, metrics.

Foreign policy positions matter, but will only influence others if they form a coherent strategic vision reinforcing principles and norms aligned with shared interests. Economic policies affect all Americans, but what will matter above all is whether net expenditures and revenues — and growth — point the country toward, or away from, future solvency. Ethics is a third pillar of sound government, as any perception of self-dealing in public service is corrosive to legitimacy, here as elsewhere.

There is a fourth metric that receives far less attention from correspondents and commentators than strategy, economics, or ethics, and that is management. The president is responsible for 440 federal departments, agencies, and sub-agencies, according to the Federal Register. The federal government employs over 2.8 million civilian employees and more than 2 million members of the armed forces, active and reserve. Among the attributes voters should seek in a president is the ability to enlist a capable leadership team and manage this vast enterprise well.

Politics aside, no one can dispute that management concerns have arisen in recent years across the federal space: waiting lines at Department of Veterans Affairs medical facilities, cyber breaches at Office of Personnel Management, Medicare fraud, troubling incidents with the Secret Service, alleged political bias by the Internal Revenue Service, the Obamacare website rollout, and others. In the national security sector, investigations have harshly critiqued major assistance projects in Afghanistan; "serious, systemic problems" within the State Department were a key finding of the Benghazi Accountability Review Board; and moves by Russia, Iran, the Islamic State, and others seem to have caught policymakers by surprise, raising questions about gaps in U.S. intelligence.

It is increasingly apparent that the same old mix of declaratory policies, consultation with other governments, and assistance resources is generating diminishing returns for America's reputation and influence. The remedy may not be new policies or more resources. In Washington today we have an overabundance of policy inputs. We also have an overabundance of policy offices, policy officials, and policy processes. The organizational charts for the key national security entities — State Department, Office of the Secretary of Defense, National Security Council Staff, Office of the Joint Chiefs, and the Intelligence Community — have in recent years exploded with new subcabinet positions, specialty offices, and staff.

Concerns arising over one issue after another have been addressed by adding to the bureaucracy: new issue-specific offices, special coordinators, and Senate-confirmed positions. With every new office or official added to the ranks, all other offices lose a little influence. In the State Department today, Secretary John Kerry has the following positions reporting to him: two deputies, six under secretaries, over 60 bureaus and offices, 18 special envoys, 18 representatives, six ambassadors-at-large, 14 issue-specific coordinators, and seven special advisors — all this before considering U.S. ambassadors abroad. No business school in the world can cite an optimally functioning organization with so many direct reporting channels to the top executive. Indeed, as one Asian former diplomat has noted, where most governments take 20 percent of the time developing policy and 80 percent implementing it, in Washington these numbers are reversed.

As hard as it is today for an innovative proposal within the State Department to gain building-wide concurrence and reach the secretary's desk, the chances that it will reach the president are further complicated by a National Security Council staff that is today more than five times larger than, for example, when Colin Powell ran the Council for President Ronald Reagan. One could cite similar expansions of staffs at military combatant commands, and on both the military and civilian sides of the Pentagon. The Directorate of National Intelligence, created post-9/11, added hundreds of personnel to "manage" the Intelligence Community.

With "1,000 bowls of rice" vying for resources, authority, and authorship of policy, one can understand why President Barack Obama has often relied on a tight circle of trusted White House aides rather than expecting the interagency to provide consistent and timely policy responses to world events.

This is a hard issue for Congress as well as the Executive Branch. All of the responsibilities reposed in single-purpose offices lead to more subcommittees of the House and Senate charged with oversight. What will it take for both branches to give up some titles, consolidate offices, streamline decision processes, and increase unity of effort in pursuit of American interests?

The answer must include a chief executive committed to mastering the management challenge. Sound strategy, budgetary discipline, and uncompromising ethics are essential, but hopes for a brighter future will be more realistic if the captain can run an effective ship of state.

Photo credit: ULRICH BAUMGARTEN via Getty Images

* * * * * *